FRÉDÉRIC MISTRAL

LECTOR HOUSE PUBLIC DOMAIN WORKS

FRÉDÉRIC MISTRAL

CHARLES ALFRED DOWNER

ISBN: 978-93-90058-94-5

Published: 1901

LECTOR HOUSE

LECTOR HOUSE LLP
E-MAIL: lectorpublishing@gmail.com

FRÉDÉRIC MISTRAL

STUDIES IN ROMANCE PHILOLOGY AND LITERATURE

FRÉDÉRIC MISTRAL
POET AND LEADER IN PROVENCE

BY

CHARLES ALFRED DOWNER
ASSISTANT PROFESSOR IN THE FRENCH LANGUAGE AND LITERATURE
IN THE COLLEGE OF THE CITY OF NEW YORK

1901

PREFACE

This study of the poetry and life-work of the leader of the modern Provençal renaissance was submitted in partial fulfilment of the requirements for the degree of Doctor of Philosophy at Columbia University. My interest in Mistral was first awakened by an article from the pen of the great Romance philologist, Gaston Paris, which appeared in the *Revue de Paris* in October, 1894. The idea of writing the book came to me during a visit to Provence in 1897. Two years later I visited the south of France again, and had the pleasure of seeing Mistral in his own home. It is my pleasant duty to express here once again my gratitude for his kindly hospitality and for his suggestions in regard to works upon the history of the Félibrige. Not often does he who studies the works of a poet in a foreign tongue enjoy as I did the privilege of hearing the verse from the poet's own lips. It was an hour not to be forgotten, and the beauty of the language has been for me since then as real as that of music finely rendered, and the force of the poet's personality was impressed upon me as it scarcely could have been even from a most sympathetic and searching perusal of his works. His great influence in southern France and his great personal popularity are not difficult to understand when one has seen the man.

As the striking fact in the works of this Frenchman is that they are not written in French, but in Provençal, a considerable portion of the present essay is devoted to the language itself. But it did not appear fitting that too much space should be devoted to the purely linguistic side of the subject. There is a field here for a great deal of special study, and the results of such investigations will be embodied in special works by those who make philological studies their special province. In the first division of the present work, however, along with the life of the poet and the history of the Félibrige, a description of the language is given, which is an account at least of its distinctive features. A short chapter will be found devoted to the subject of the versification of the poets who write in the new speech. This subject is not treated in Koschwitz's admirable grammar of the language.

The second division is devoted to the poems. The epics of Mistral, if we may venture to use the term, are, with the exception of Lamartine's *Jocelyn*, the most remarkable long narrative poems that have been produced in France in modern times. At least one of them would appear to be a work of the highest rank and destined to live. Among the short poems that constitute the volume called *Lis Isclo d'Or* are a number of masterpieces.

This book aims to present all the essential facts in the history of this astonishing revival of a language, and to bring out the chief aspects of Mistral's life-work. In our conclusions we have not yielded to the temptation to prophesy. The conflicting tendencies of cosmopolitanism and nationalism abroad in the world to-day give rise to fascinating speculations as to the future. In the Felibrean movement we have a very interesting problem of this kind, and no one can terminate a study of the subject without asking himself the question, "What is going to come out of it all?" No one can tell, and so we have not ventured beyond the attempt to present the case as it actually exists.

Let me here also offer an expression of gratitude to Professor Adolphe Cohn and to Professor Henry A. Todd of Columbia University for their advice and guidance during the past six years. Their kindness and the inspiration of their example must be reckoned among those things that cannot be repaid.

NEW YORK, March, 1901.

CONTENTS

CONTENTS

ix

PART FIRST
THE REVIVAL OF THE PROVENÇAL LANGUAGE

CHAPTER I
INTRODUCTION LIFE OF MISTRAL

The present century has witnessed a remarkable literary phenomenon in the south of France, a remarkable rebirth of local patriotism. A language has been born again, so to speak, and once more, after a sleep of many hundred years, the sunny land that was the cradle of modern literature, offers us a new efflorescence of poetry, embodied in the musical tongue that never has ceased to be spoken on the soil where the Troubadours sang of love. Those who began this movement knew not whither they were tending. From small beginnings, out of a kindly desire to give the humbler folk a simple, homely literature in the language of their firesides, there grew a higher ambition. The Provençal language put forth claims to exist coequally with the French tongue on French soil. Memories of the former glories of the southern regions of France began to stir within the hearts of the modern poets and leaders. They began to chafe under the strong political and intellectual centralization that prevails in France, and to seek to bring about a change. The movement has passed through numerous phases, has been frequently misinterpreted and misunderstood, and may now, after it has attained to tangible results, be defined as an aim, on the part of its leaders, to make the south intellectually independent of Paris. It is an attempt to restore among the people of the Rhone region a love of their ancient customs, language, and traditions, an effort to raise a sort of dam against the flood of modern tendencies that threaten to overwhelm local life. These men seek to avoid that dead level of uniformity to which the national life of France appears to them in danger of sinking. In the earlier days, the leaders of this movement were often accused at Paris of a spirit of political separatism; they were actually mistrusted as secessionists, and certain it is that among them have been several champions of the idea of decentralization. To-day there are found in their ranks a few who advocate the federal idea in the political organization of France. However, there seems never to have been a time when the movement promised seriously to bring about practical political changes; and whatever political significance it may have to-day goes no farther than what may be contained in germ in the effort at an intense local life.

The land of the Troubadours is now the land of the Félibres; these modern singers do not forget, nor will they allow the people of the south to forget, that the union of France with Provence was that of an equal with an equal, not of a principal with a subordinate. Patriots they are, however, ardent lovers of France, and proofs of their strong affection for their country are not wanting. To-day, amid all their activity and demonstrations in behalf of what they often call *"la petite patrie,"* no enemies or doubters are found to question their loyalty to the greater father-land.

The movement began in the revival of the Provençal language, and was at first a very modest attempt to make it serve merely better purposes than it had done after the eclipse that followed the Albigensian war. For a long time the linguistic and literary aspect of all this activity was the only one that attracted any attention in the rest of France or in Provence itself. Not that the Provençal language had ever quite died out even as a written language. Since the days of the Troubadours there had been a continuous succession of writers in the various dialects of southern France, but very few of them were men of power and talent. Among the immediate predecessors of the Félibres must be mentioned Saboly, whose *Noëls*, or Christmas songs, are to-day known all over the region, and Jasmin, who, however, wrote in a different dialect. Jasmin's fame extended far beyond the limited audience for which he wrote; his work came to the attention of the cultured through the enthusiastic praise of Sainte-Beuve, and he is to-day very widely known. The English-speaking world became acquainted with him chiefly through the translations of Longfellow. Jasmin, however, looked upon himself as the last of a line, and when, in his later years, he heard of the growing fame of the new poets of the Rhone country, it is said he looked upon them with disfavor, if not jealousy. Strange to say, he was, in the early days, unknown to those whose works, like his, have now attained well-nigh world-wide celebrity.

The man who must justly be looked upon as the father of the present movement was Joseph Roumanille. He was born in 1818, in the little town of Saint-Rémy, a quaint old place, proud of some remarkable Roman remains, situated to the south of Avignon. Roumanille was far from foreseeing the consequences of the impulse he had given in arousing interest in the old dialect, and, until he beheld the astonishing successes of Mistral, strongly disapproved the ambitions of a number of his fellow-poets to seek an audience for their productions outside of the immediate region. He had no more ambitious aim than to raise the patois of Saint-Rémy out of the veritable mire into which it had sunk; it pained him to see that the speech of his fireside was never used in writing except for trifles and obscenities. Of him is told the touching story that one day, while reciting in his home before a company of friends some poems in French that he had written, he observed tears in his mother's eyes. She could not understand the poetry his friends so much admired. Roumanille, much moved, resolved to write no verses that his mother could not enjoy, and henceforth devoted himself ardently to the task of purifying and perfecting the dialect of Saint-Rémy. It has been said, no less truthfully than poetically, that from a mother's tear was born the new Provençal poetry, destined to so splendid a career.

We of the English-speaking race are apt to wonder at this love of a local dialect. This vigorous attempt to create a first-rate literature, alongside and independent of the national literature, seems strange or unnatural. We are accustomed to one language, spoken over immense areas, and we rejoice to see it grow and spread, more and more perfectly unified. With all their local color, in spite of their expression of provincial or colonial life, the writings of a Kipling are read and enjoyed wherever the English language has penetrated. In Italy we find patriots and writers working with utmost energy to bring into being a really national language. Nearly all the governments of Europe seek to impose the language of the capital upon the schools. Unification of language seems a most desirable thing, and, superficially considered, the tendency would appear to be in that direction. But the truth is that there exists all over Europe a war of tongues. The Welsh, the Basques, the Norwegians, the Bohemians, the Finns, the Hungarians, are of one mind with Daudet and Mistral, who both express the sentiment, "He who holds to his language, holds the key of his prison."

So Roumanille loved and cherished the melodious speech of the Rhone valley. He hoped to see the *langue d'oc* saved from destruction, he strove against the invasion of the northern speech that threatened to overwhelm it. He wrote sweet verses and preached the gospel of the home-speech. One day he discovered a boy whom he calls "l'enfant sublime," and the pupil soon carried his dreams to a realization far beyond his fondest hopes. Not Roumanille, but Frédéric Mistral has made the new Provençal literature what it is. In him were combined all the qualities, all the powers requisite for the task, and the task grew with time. It became more than a question of language. Mistral soon came to seek not only the creation of an independent literature, he aimed at nothing less than a complete revolution, or rather a complete rebirth, of the mental life of southern France. Provence was to save her individuality entire. Geographically at the central point of the lands inhabited by the so-called Latin races, she was to regain her ancient prominence, and cause the eyes of her sisters to turn her way once more with admiration and affection. The patois of Saint-Rémy has been developed and expanded into a beautiful literary language. The inertia of the Provençals themselves has been overcome. There is undoubtedly a new intellectual life in the Rhone valley, and the fame of the Félibres and their great work has gone abroad into distant lands.

The purpose, then, of the present dissertation, will be to give an account of the language of the Félibres, and to examine critically the literary work of their acknowledged chief and guiding spirit, Frédéric Mistral.

The story of his life he himself has told most admirably in the preface to the first edition of *Lis Isclo d'Or*, published at Avignon in 1874. He was born in 1830, on the 8th day of September, at Maillane. Maillane is a village, near Saint-Rémy, situated in the centre of a broad plain that lies at the foot of the Alpilles, the westernmost rocky heights of the Alps. Here the poet is still living, and here he has passed his life almost uninterruptedly. His father's home was a little way out of the village, and the boy was brought up at the *mas*,[1] amid farm-hands and shepherds. His father had married a second time at the age of fifty-five, and our poet was the only child of this second marriage.

The story of the first meeting of his parents is thus told by the poet:—

"One year, on St. John's day, Maître François Mistral was in the midst of his wheat, which a company of harvesters were reaping. A throng of young girls,

---

[1] The word *mas*, which is kin with the English *manse* and *mansion*, signifies the home in the country with numerous outbuildings grouped closely about it.

gleaning, followed the reapers and raked up the ears that fell. Maître François (Mèste Francés in Provençal), my father, noticed a beautiful girl that remained behind as if she were ashamed to glean like the others. He drew near and said to her:—

"'My child, whose daughter are you? What is your name?'

"The young girl replied, 'I am the daughter of Etienne Poulinet, Maire of Maillane. My name is Délaïde.'

"'What! the daughter of the Maire of Maillane gleaning!'

"'Maître,' she replied, 'our family is large, six girls and two boys, and although our father is pretty well to do, as you know, when we ask him for money to dress with, he answers, "Girls, if you want finery, earn it!" And that is why I came to glean.'

"Six months after this meeting, which reminds one of the ancient scene of Ruth and Boaz, Maître François asked Maître Poulinet for the hand of Délaïde, and I was born of that marriage."

His father's lands were extensive, and a great number of men were required to work them. The poem, *Mirèio*, is filled with pictures of the sort of life led in the country of Maillane. Of his father he says that he towered above them all, in stature, in wisdom, and in nobleness of bearing. He was a handsome old man, dignified in language, firm in command, kind to the poor about him, austere with himself alone. The same may be said of the poet to-day. He is a strikingly handsome man, vigorous and active, exceedingly gracious and simple in manner. His utter lack of affectation is the more remarkable, in view of the fact that he has been for years an object of adulation, and lives in constant and close contact with a population of peasants.

His schooling began at the age of nine, but the boy played truant so frequently that he was sent to boarding-school in Avignon. Here he had a sad time of it, and seems especially to have felt the difference of language. Teachers and pupils alike made fun of his patois, for which he had a strong attachment, because of the charm of the songs his mother sung to him. Later he studied well, however, and became filled with a love of Virgil and Homer. In them he found pictures of life that recalled vividly the labors, the ways, and the ideas of the Maillanais. At this time, too, he attempted a translation, in Provençal, of the first eclogue of Virgil, and confided his efforts to a school-mate, Anselme Mathieu, who became his life-long friend and one of the most active among the Félibres.

It was at this school, in 1845, that he formed his friendship with Roumanille, who had come there as a teacher. It is not too much to say that the revival of the Provençal language grew out of this meeting. Roumanille had already written his poems, *Li Margarideto* (The Daisies). "Scarcely had he shown me," says Mistral, "in their spring-time freshness, these lovely field-flowers, when a thrill ran through my being and I exclaimed, 'This is the dawn my soul awaited to awaken to the light!'" Mistral had read some Provençal, but at that time the dialect was employed merely in derision; the writers used the speech itself as the chief comic element in their productions. The poems of Jasmin were as yet unknown to him. Roumanille was the first in the Rhone country to sing the poetry of the heart. Master and pupil became firm friends and worked together for years to raise the home-speech to the dignity of a literary language.

At seventeen Mistral returned home, and began a poem in four cantos, that he has never published; though portions of it are among the poems of *Lis Isclo d'Or* and in the notes of *Mirèio*. This poem is called *Li Meissoun* (Harvest). His family, seeing his intellectual superiority, sent him to Aix to study law. Here he again met Mathieu, and they made up for the aridity of the Civil Code by devoting themselves to poetry in Provençal.

In 1851 the young man returned to the *mas*, a *licencié en droit*, and his father said to him: "Now, my dear son, I have done my duty; you know more than ever I learned. Choose your career; I leave you free." And the poet tells us he threw his lawyer's gown to the winds and gave himself up to the contemplation of what he so loved,—the splendor of his native Provence.

Through Roumanille he came to know Aubanel, Croustillat, and others. They met at Avignon, full of youthful enthusiasm, and during this period Mistral, encouraged by his friends, worked upon his greatest poem, *Mirèio*. In 1854, on the 21st of May, the Félibrige was founded by the seven poets,—Joseph Roumanille, Paul Giéra, Théodore Aubanel, Eugène Garcin, Anselme Mathieu, Frédéric Mistral, Alphonse Tavan. In 1868, Garcin published a violent attack upon the Félibres, accusing them, in the strongest language, of seeking to bring about a political separation of southern France from the rest of the country. This apostasy was a cause of great grief to the others, and Garcin's name was stricken from the official list of the founders of the Félibrige, and replaced by that of Jean Brunet. Mistral, in the sixth canto of *Mirèio*, addresses in eloquent verse his comrades in the Provençal Pléiade, and there we still find the name of Garcin.

> Tù' nfin, de quau un vènt de flamo
> Ventoulo, emporto e fouito l'amo
> Garcin, o fiéu ardènt dóu manescau d'Alen!

(And finally, thou whose soul is stirred and swept and whipped by a wind of flame, Garcin, ardent son of the smith of Alleins.)

This attack upon the Félibrige was the first of the kind ever made. Many years later, Garcin became reconciled to his former friends and in 1897 he was vice-president of the *Félibrige de Paris*.

The number seven and the task undertaken by these poets and literary reformers remind us instantly of the Pléiade, whose work in the sixteenth century in attempting to perfect the French language was of a very similar character. It is certain, however, that the seven poets who inaugurated their work at the Château of Font-Ségugne, had no thought of imitating the Pléiade either in the choice of the number seven or in the reformation they were about to undertake.

They began their propaganda by founding an annual publication called the *Armana Prouvençau*, which has appeared regularly since 1855, and many of their writings were first printed in this official magazine. Of the seven, Aubanel alone besides Mistral has attained celebrity as a poet, and these two with Roumanille have been usually associated in the minds of all who have followed the movement with interest as its three leaders.

Mistral completed *Mirèio* in 1859. The poem was presented by Adolphe Dumas and Jean Reboul to Lamartine, who devoted to it one of the "Entretiens" of his *Cours familier de littérature*. This article of Lamartine, and his personal efforts on behalf of Mistral, contributed greatly to the success of the poem. Lamartine wrote among other things: "A great epic poet is born! A true Homeric poet in our own time; a poet, born like the men of Deucalion, from a stone on the Crau, a primitive poet in our decadent age; a Greek poet at Avignon; a poet who has created a language out of a dialect, as Petrarch created Italian; one who, out of a vulgar *patois*, has made a language full of imagery and harmony delighting the imagination and the ear.... We might say that, during the night, an island of the Archipelago, a floating Delos, has parted from its group of Greek or Ionian islands and come silently to join the mainland of sweet-scented Provence, bringing along one of the divine singers of the family of the Melesigenes."

Mistral went to Paris, where for a time he was the lion of the literary world. The French Academy crowned his poem, and Gounod composed the opera Mireille, which was performed for the first time in 1864, in Paris.

The poet did not remain long in the capital. He doubtless realized that he was not destined to join the galaxy of Parisian writers, and it is certain that if he had remained there his life and his influence would have been utterly different. He returned home and immediately set to work upon a second epic; in another seven years he completed *Calendau*, published in Avignon in 1866. The success of this poem was decidedly less than that of *Mirèio*.

During these years he published many of the shorter poems that appeared in one volume in 1875, under the title of *Lis Isclo d'Or* (The Golden Islands). Meanwhile the idea of the Félibrige made great progress. The language of the Félibres had now a fixed orthography and definite grammatical form. The appearance of a master-work had given a wonderful impulse. The exuberance of the southern temperament responded quickly to the call for a manifestation of patriotic enthusiasm. The Catalan poets joined their brothers beyond the Pyrenees. The Floral games were founded. The Félibrige passed westward beyond the Rhone and found adherents in all south France. The centenary of Petrarch celebrated at Avignon in 1874 tended to emphasize the importance and the glory of the new literature.

The definite organization of the Félibrige into a great society with its hierarchy of officers took place in 1876, with Mistral as *Capoulié* (Chief or President). In this same year also the poet married Mdlle. Marie Rivière of Dijon, and this lady, who was named first Queen of the Félibrige by Albert de Quintana of Catalonia, the poet-laureate of the year 1878 at the great Floral Games held in Montpellier, has become at heart and in speech a Provençale.

A third poem, *Nerto*, appeared in 1884, and showed the poet in a new light; his admirers now compared him to Ariosto. This same year he made a second journey to Paris, and was again the lion of the hour. The *Société de la Cigale*, which had been founded in 1876, as a Paris branch of the Félibrige, and which later became the *Société des Félibres de Paris*, organized banquets and festivities in his honor, and celebrated the Floral Games at Sceaux to commemorate the four hundredth anniversary of the day when Provence became united, of her own free-will, with France. Mistral was received with distinction by President Grévy and by the Count of Paris, and his numerous Parisian friends vied in bidding him welcome to the capital. His new poem was crowned by the French Academy, receiving the Prix Vitet, the presentation address being delivered by Legouvé. Four years later, *Lou Tresor dóu Felibrige*, a great dictionary of all the dialects of the *langue d'oc*, was completed, and in 1890 appeared his only dramatic work, *La Rèino Jano* (Queen Joanna). In 1897 he produced his last long poem, epic in form, *Lou Pouèmo dóu Rose* (the Poem of the Rhone). At present he is engaged upon his *Memoirs*.

Aside from his rare journeys to Paris, a visit to Switzerland, and another to Italy, Mistral has rarely gone beyond the borders of his beloved region. He is still living quietly in the little village of Maillane, in a simple but beautiful home, surrounded with works of art inspired by the Felibrean movement. He has survived many of his distinguished friends. Roumanille, Mathieu, Aubanel, Daudet, and Paul Arène have all passed away; a new generation is about him. But his activity knows no rest. The Felibrean festivities continue, the numerous publications in the Provençal tongue still have in him a constant contributor. In 1899 the Museon Arlaten (the Museum of Aries) was inaugurated, and is another proof of the constant energy and enthusiasm of the poet. He is to-day the greatest man in the south of France, universally beloved and revered.

His life after all has been less a literary life than one of direct and unceasing personal action upon the population about him. The resurrection of the language, the publication of poems, magazines, and newspapers, are only part of a programme tending to raise the people of the south to a conception of their individuality as a race. He has striven untiringly to communicate to them his own glowing enthusiasm for the past glories of Provence, to fire them with his dream of a great rebirth of the Latin races, to lay the foundation of a great ideal Latin union. Wonderful is his optimism. Some of the Félibres about him are somewhat discouraged, many of them have never set their aspirations as high as he has done, and some look upon his dreams as Utopian. Whatever be the future of the movement he has founded, Mistral's life in its simple oneness, and in its astonishing success, is indeed most remarkable. Provence, the land that first gave the world a literature after the decay of the classic tongues, has awakened again under his magic touch to an active mental life. A second literature is in active being on the soil of France, a second literary language is there a reality. Whether permanent or evanescent, this glorification of poetry, this ardent love of the beautiful and the ideal, is a noble and inspiring spectacle amid the turmoil and strife of this age of material progress.

CHAPTER II
THE FÉLIBRIGE

The history of the Félibrige, from its beginning, in 1854, down to the year 1896, has been admirably written by G. Jourdanne.[2] The work is quite exhaustive, containing, in addition to the excellently written narrative, an engraving of the famous cup, portraits of all the most noted Félibres, a series of elaborately written notes that discuss or set forth many questions relating to the general theme, a very large bibliography of the subject, comprising long lists of works that have been written in the dialect or that have appeared in France and in other countries concerning the Félibres, a copy of the constitution of the society and of various statutes relating to it. It not only contains all the material that is necessary for the study of the Félibrige, but it is worthy of the highest praise for the spirit in which it is written. It is an honest attempt to explain the Félibrige, and to present fairly and fully all the problems that so remarkable a movement has created. A perusal of the book makes it evident that the author believes in future political consequences, and while well aware that it is unsafe to prophesy, he has a chapter on the future of the movement.

His history endeavors to show that the Felibrean renaissance was not a spontaneous springing into existence. On the purely literary side, however, it certainly bears the character of a creation; as writers, the Provençal poets may scarcely be said to continue any preceding school or to be closely linked with any literary past. In its inception it was a mere attempt to write pleasing, popular verse of a better kind in the dialect of the fireside. But the movement developed rapidly into the ambition to endow the whole region with a real literature, to awaken a consciousness of *race* in the men of the south; these aims have been realized, and a change has come over the life of Provence and the land of the *langue d'oc* in general. The author believes and adduces evidences to show that all this could not have come about had the seed not fallen upon a soil that was ready.

The Félibrige dates from the year 1854, but the idea that lies at the bottom of it must be traced back to the determination of Roumanille to write in Provençal rather than in French. He produced his *Margarideto* in 1847 and the *Sounjarello* in 1851. In collaboration with Mistral and Anselme Mathieu, he edited a collection of poems by living writers under the title *Li Prouvençalo*. During these years, too, there were meetings of Provençal writers for the purpose of discussing questions of grammar and spelling. These meetings, including even the historic one of May 21, 1854, were, however, really little more than friendly, social gatherings, where a

[2] *Histoire du Félibrige, par* G. Jourdanne, *Librairie Roumanille, Avignon, 1897.*

number of enthusiastic friends sang songs and made merry. They had none of the solemnity of a conclave, or the dignity of literary assemblies. There was no formal organization. Those writers who were zealously interested in the rehabilitation of the Provençal speech and connected themselves with Mistral and his friends were the Félibres. Not until 1876 was there a Félibrige with a formal constitution and an elaborate organization.

The word *Félibre* was furnished by Mistral, who had come upon it in an old hymn wherein occurs the expression that the Virgin met Jesus in the temple among "the seven Félibres of the law." The origin and etymology of this word have given rise to various explanations. The Greek *philabros*, lover of the beautiful; *philebraios*, lover of Hebrew, hence, among the Jews, teacher; *felibris*, nursling, according to Ducange; the Irish *filea*, bard, and *ber*, chief, have been proposed. Jeanroy (in *Romania*, XIII, p. 463) offers the etymology: Spanish *feligres, filii Ecclesiæ*, sons of the church, parishioners. None of these is certain.

Seven poets were present at this first meeting, and as the day happened to be that of St. Estelle, the emblem of a seven-pointed star was adopted. Very fond of the number seven are these Félibres; they tell you of the seven chief churches of Avignon, its seven gates, seven colleges, seven hospitals, seven popes who were there seventy years; the word *Félibre* has seven letters, so has Mistral's name, and he spent seven years in writing each of his epics.

The task that lay before these poets was twofold: they had not only to prune and purify their dialect and produce verses, they had also to find readers, to create a public, to begin a propaganda. The first means adopted was the publication of the *Armana prouvençau*, already referred to. In 1855, five hundred copies were issued, in 1894, twelve thousand. For four years this magazine was destined for Provence alone; in 1860, after the appearance of *Mirèio*, it was addressed to all the dwellers in southern France. The great success of *Mirèio* began a new period in the history of the Félibrige. Mistral himself and the poets about him now took an entirely new view of their mission. The uplifting of the people, the creation of a literature that should be admired abroad as well as at home, the complete expression of the life of Provence, in all its aspects, past and present, escape from the implacable centralization that tends to destroy all initiative and originality—such were the higher aims toward which they now bent their efforts. The attention of Paris was turned in their direction. Jasmin had already shown the Parisians that real poetry of a high order could be written in a patois. Lamartine and Villemain welcomed the new literature most cordially, and the latter declared that "France is rich enough to have two literatures."

But the student of this history must not lose sight of the fact that the Provençal poets are not first of all littérateurs; they are not men devoting themselves to literature for a livelihood, or even primarily for fame. They are patriots before they are poets. The choice of subjects and the intense love of their native land that breathes through all their writings, are ample proof of this. They meet to sing songs and to speak; it is always of Provence that they sing and speak. Almost all of them are men who ply some trade, hardly one lives by his pen alone. This fact gives a very special character to their whole production. The Felibrean movement is more than an astonishing literary phenomenon.

The idea from this time on acquired more and more adherents. Scores of writers appeared, and volumes whose titles filled many pages swelled the output of Provençal verse. These new aims were due to the success of *Mirèio*; but it must not be forgotten that Mistral himself, in that poem and in the shorter poems of the same period, gave distinct expression to the new order of ideas, so that we are constantly led back to him, in all our study of the matter, as the creator, the continuer, and the ever present inspirer of the Félibrige. Whatever it is, it is through him primarily. Roumanille must be classed as one of those precursors who are unconscious of what they do. To him the Félibres owe two things: first of all, the idea of writing in the dialect works of literary merit; and, secondly, the discovery of Frédéric Mistral.

Among these new ideas, one that dominates henceforth in the story of the Félibrige, is the idea of race. Mistral is well aware that there is no Latin race, in the sense of blood relationship, of physical descent; he knows that the so-called Latin race has, for the base of its unity, a common history, a common tradition, a common religion, a common language.

But he believes that there is a *race méridionale* that has been developed into a kind of unity out of the various elements that compose it, through their being mingled together, and accumulating during many centuries common memories, ideas, customs, and interests. So Mistral has devoted himself to promoting knowledge of its history, traditions, language, and religion. As the Félibrige grew, and as Mistral felt his power as a poet grow, he sought a larger public; he turned naturally to the peoples most closely related to his own, and Italy and Spain were embraced in his sympathies. The Félibrige spread beyond the limits of France first into Spain. Victor Balaguer, exiled from his native country, was received with open arms by the Provençals. William Bonaparte-Wyse, an Irishman and a grand-nephew of the first Napoleon, while on a journey through Provence, had become converted to the Felibrean doctrines, and became an active spirit among these poets and orators. He organized a festival in honor of Balaguer, and when, later, the Catalan poet was permitted to return home, the Catalans sent the famous cup to their friends in Provence. For the Félibres this cup is an emblem of the idea of a Latin federation, and as it passes from hand to hand and from lip to lip at the Felibrean banquets, the scene is not unlike that wherein the Holy Graal passes about among the Knights of the Round Table.[3]

Celebrations of this kind have become a regular institution in southern France.

[3] The stem of the cup has the form of a palm tree, under which two female figures, representing Catalonia and Provence, stand in a graceful embrace. Below the figures are engraved the two following inscriptions:—

Morta la diuhen qu'es,	Ah! se me sabien entèndre!
Mes jo la crech viva.	Ah! se me voulien segui!
(V. Balaguer.)	(F. Mistral.)
(They say she is dead,	(Ah, if they could understand me!
but I believe she lives.)	Ah, if they would follow me!)

Since the day in 1862 when the town of Apt received the Félibres officially, organizing Floral Games, in which prizes were offered for the best poems in Provençal, the people have become accustomed to the sight of these triumphal entries of the poets into their cities. Reports of these brilliant festivities have gone abroad into all lands. If the love of noise and show that characterizes the southern temperament has caused these reunions to be somewhat unfavorably criticised as theatrical, on the other hand the enthusiasm has been genuine, and the results real and lasting. The *Félibrées*, so they are called, have not all taken place in France. In 1868, Mistral, Rournieux, Bonaparte-Wyse, and Paul Meyer went to Barcelona, where they were received with great pomp and ceremony. Men eminent in literary and philological circles in Paris have often accepted invitations to these festivities. In 1876, a Felibrean club, "La Cigale," was founded in the capital; its first president was Henri de Bornier, author of *La Fille de Roland*. Professors and students of literature and philology in France and in other countries began to interest themselves in the Félibres, and the Félibrige to-day counts among its members men of science as well as men of letters.

In 1874 one of the most remarkable of the celebrations, due to the initiative of M. de Berluc-Pérussis, was held at Vaucluse to celebrate the fifth centenary of the death of Petrarch. At this *Félibrée* the Italians first became affiliated to the *idea*, and the Italian ambassador, Nigra, the president of the Accademia della Crusca, Signor Conti, and Professor Minich, from the University of Padua, were the delegates. The Institute of France was represented for the first time. This celebration was highly important and significant, and the scenes of Petrarch's inspirations and the memories of the founder of the Renaissance must have awakened responsive echoes in the hearts of the poets who aimed at a second rebirth of poetry and learning in the same region.

The following year the *Société des langues romanes* at Montpellier offered prizes for philological as well as purely literary works, and for the first time other dialects than the Provençal proper were admitted in the competitions. The Languedocian, the Gascon, the Limousin, the Béarnais, and the Catalan dialects were thus included. The members of the jury were men of the greatest note, Gaston Paris, Michel Bréal, Mila y Fontanals, being of their number.

Finally, in 1876, on the 21st of May, the statutes of the Félibrige were adopted. From them we quote the following:—

"The Félibrige is established to bring together and encourage all those who, by their works, preserve the language of the land of *oc*, as well as the men of science and the artists who study and work in the interest of this country."

"Political and religious discussions are forbidden in the Felibrean meetings."

The organization is interesting. The Félibres are divided into *Majoraux* and *Mainteneurs*. The former are limited to fifty in number, and form the Consistory, which elects its own members; new members are received on the feast of St. Estelle.

The Consistory is presided over by a Capoulié, who wears as the emblem of his office a seven-pointed golden star, the other Majoraux, a golden grasshopper.

The other Félibres are unlimited in number. Any seven Félibres dwelling in the same place may ask the Maintenance to form them into a school. The schools administer their own affairs.

Every seven years the Floral Games are held, at which prizes are distributed; every year, on the feast of St. Estelle, a general meeting of the Félibrige takes place. Each Maintenance must meet once a year.

At the Floral Games he who is crowned poet-laureate chooses the Queen, and she crowns him with a wreath of olive leaves.

To-day there are three Maintenances within the limits of French soil, Provence, Languedoc, Aquitaine.

Among other facts that should doubtless be reported here is, the list of Capouliés. They have been Mistral (1876-1888), Roumanille (1888-1891), and Félix Gras; the Queens have been Madame Mistral, Mlle. Thérèse Roumanille, Mlle. Marie Girard, and the Comtesse Marie-Thérèse de Chevigné, who is descended upon her mother's side from Laura de Sade, generally believed to be Petrarch's Laura.

Since the organization went into effect the Félibrige has expanded in many ways, its influence has continually grown, new questions have arisen. Among these last have been burning questions of religion and politics, for although discussions of them are banished from Felibrean meetings, opinions of the most various kind exist among the Félibres, have found expression, and have well-nigh resulted in difficulties. Until 1876 these questions slept. Mistral is a Catholic, but has managed to hold more or less aloof from political matters. Aubanel was a zealous Catholic, and had the title by inheritance of Printer to his Holiness. Roumanille was a Catholic, and an ardent Royalist. When the Félibrige came to extend its limits over into Languedoc, the poet Auguste Fourès and his fellows proclaimed a different doctrine, and called up memories of the past with a different view. They affirmed their adherence to the *Renaissance méridionale*, and claimed equal rights for the Languedocian dialect. They asserted, however, that the true tradition was republican, and protested vigorously against the clerical and monarchical parties, which, in their opinion, had always been for Languedoc a cause of disaster, servitude, and misery. The memory of the terrible crusade in the thirteenth century inspired fiery poems among them. Hatred of Simon de Montfort and of the invaders who followed him, free-thought, and federalism found vigorous expression in all their productions. In Provence, too, there have been opinions differing widely from those of the original founders, and the third Capoulié, Félix Gras, was a Protestant. Of him M. Jourdanne writes:—

"Finally, in 1891, after the death of Roumanille, the highest office in the Félibrige was taken by a man who could rally about him the two elements that we have seen manifested, sufficiently Republican to satisfy the most ardent in the extreme Left, sufficiently steady not to alarm the Royalists, a great enough poet to deserve without any dispute the first place in an assembly of poets."

He, like Mistral, wrote epics in twelve cantos. His first work, *Li Carbounié*, has on its title-page three remarkable lines:—

"I love my village more than thy village,
I love my Provence more than thy province,
I love France more than all."

Possibly no other three lines could express as well the whole spirit of the Félibrige.

Our subject being Mistral and not Félix Gras, a passing mention must suffice. One of his remarkable works is called *Toloza*, and recounts the crusade of the Albigenses, and his novel, *The Reds of the Midi*, first published in New York in the English translation of Mrs. Thomas A. Janvier, is probably the most remarkable prose work that has been written in Provençal.[4] Only the future can tell whether the Provençal will pass through a prose cycle after its poetic cycle, in the manner of all literatures. To many serious thinkers the attempt to create a complete literature seems of very doubtful success.

The problems, then, which confront the Félibres are numerous. Can they, with any assurance of permanence, maintain two literary languages in the same region? It is scarcely necessary to state, of course, that no one dreams of supplanting the French language anywhere on French soil. What attitude shall they assume toward the "patoisants," that is, those who insist on using the local dialect, and refuse to conform to the usage of the Félibres? Is it not useless, after all, to hope for a more perfect unification of the dialects of the *langue d'oc*, and, if unification is the aim, does not logical reasoning lead to the conclusion that the French language already exists, perfectly unified, and absolutely necessary? In the matter of politics, the most serious questions may arise if the desires of some find more general favor. Shall the Félibres aim at local self-government, at a confederation something like that of the Swiss cantons? Shall they advocate the idea of independent universities?

As a matter of fact, none of these problems are solved, and they will only be solved by the natural march of events. The attitude of the leaders toward all these differing views has become one of easy toleration. If the language of the Félibres tends already to dominate the other dialects, if its influence is already plainly felt far beyond Provence itself, this is due to the sheer superiority of their literary work. If their literature had the conventional character of that of the Troubadours, if it were addressed exclusively to a certain élite, then their language might have been adopted by the poets of other regions, just as in the days of the Troubadours the masters of the art of "trobar" preferred to use the Limousin dialect. But the popular character of the movement has prevented this. It has preached the love of the village, and each locality, as fast as the Felibrean idea gained ground, has shown greater affection for its own dialect.

Mistral's work has often been compared to Dante's. But Dante did not impose his language upon Italy by the sole superiority of his great poem. All sorts of events, political and social, contributed to the result, and there is little reason to expect the same future for the work of Mistral. This comparison is made from the

____

[4] In 1899, Félix Gras published a novel called *The White Terror*. His death occurred early in 1901.

linguistic point of view; it is not likely that any one will compare the two as poets. At most, it may be said that if Dante gave expression to the whole spirit of his age, Mistral has given complete expression to the spirit of his little *patrie*. Should the trend of events lead to a further unification of the dialects of southern France, there is no doubt that the Felibrean dialect has by far the greatest chance of success.

The people of Provence owe a great debt to the Félibres, who have endowed them with a literature that comes closer to their sympathies than the classic literature of France can ever come; they have been raised in their own esteem, and there has been undoubtedly a great awakening in their mental life. The Félibrige has given expression to all that is noblest and best in the race, and has invariably led onward and upward. Its mission has been one that commands respect and admiration, and the Félibres to-day are in a position to point with pride to the great work accomplished among their people. Arsène Darmesteter has well said:—

"A nation needs poetry; it lives not by bread alone, but in the ideal as well. Religious beliefs are weakening; and if the sense of poetic ideals dies along with the religious sentiment, there will remain nothing among the lower classes but material and brutal instincts.

"Whether the Félibres were conscious of this danger, or met this popular need instinctively, I cannot say. At any rate, their work is a good one and a wholesome one. There still circulates, down to the lowest stratum of the people, a stream of poetry, often obscure, until now looked upon with disdain by all except scholars. I mean folklore, beliefs, traditions, legends, and popular tales. Before this source of poetry could disappear completely, the Félibres had the happy idea of taking it up, giving it a new literary form, thus giving back to the people, clothed in the brilliant colors of poetry, the creation of the people themselves."

And again: "As for this general renovation of popular poetry, I would give it no other name than that of the Félibrige. To the Félibres is due the honor of the movement; it is their ardor and their faith that have developed and strengthened it."

CHAPTER III

THE MODERN PROVENÇAL, OR, MORE ACCURATELY, THE LANGUAGE OF THE FÉLIBRES

The language of the Félibres is based upon the dialect spoken in the plain of Maillane, in and about the town of Saint-Rémy. This dialect is one of the numerous divisions of the *langue d'oc*, which Mistral claims is spoken by nearly twelve millions of people. The literary history of these patois has been written by B. Noulet, and shows that at the close of the terrible struggles of the Albigenses the language seemed dead. In 1324 seven poets attempted to found at Toulouse the competitions of the *Gai Savoir*, and so to revive the ancient poetry and the ancient language. Their attempt failed. There was literary production of varying degree of merit throughout two or three centuries; but until the time of Jasmin no writer attracted any attention beyond his immediate vicinity; and it is significant that the Félibres themselves were long in ignorance of Jasmin. It is then not difficult to demonstrate that the Félibrige revival bears more the character of a creation than of an evolution. It is not at all an evolution of the literature of the Troubadours; it is in no way like it. The language of the Félibres is not even the descendant of the special dialect that dominated as a literary language in the days of the Troubadours; for it was the speech of Limousin that formed the basis of that language, and only two of the greater poets among the Troubadours, Raimond de Vaqueiras and Fouquet de Marseille, were natives of Provence proper.

The dialect of Saint-Rémy is simply one of countless ramifications of the dialects descended from the Latin. Mistral and his associates have made their literary language out of this dialect as they found it, and not out of the language of the Troubadours. They have regularized the spelling, and have deliberately eliminated as far as possible words and forms that appeared to them to be due to French influence, substituting older and more genuine forms—forms that appeared more in accord with the genius of the *langue d'oc* as contrasted with the *langue d'oil*. Thus, *glòri, istòri, paire*, replace *gloaro, istouèro, pèro*, which are often heard among the people. This was the first step. The second step taken arose from the necessity of making this speech of the illiterate capable of elevated expression. Mistral claims to have used no word unknown to the people or unintelligible to them, with the exception that he has used freely of the stock of learned words common to the whole Romance family of languages. These words, too, he transforms more or less, keeping them in harmony with the forms peculiar to the *langue d'oc*. Hence, it is true that the language of the Félibres is a conventional, literary language, that does not represent exactly the speech of any section of France, and is related to the popular speech more or less as any official language is to the dialects that underlie it. As the Félibres themselves have received all their instruction and literary culture in the French language, they use it among themselves, and their prose especially shows the influence of the French to the extent that it may be said that the Provençal sentence, in prose, appears to be a word-for-word translation of an underlying French sentence.

Phonetically, the dialect offers certain marked differences when contrasted with French. First of all is the forceful utterance of the stressed syllable; the Provençal has post-tonic syllables, unlike the sister-speech. Here it may be said to occupy a sort of middle position between Italian and Spanish on the one hand, and French on the other; for in the former languages the accent is found in all parts of the word, in French practically only upon the final, and then it is generally weak, so that the notion of a stress is almost lost. The stress in Provençal is placed upon one of the last two syllables only, and only three vowels, *e, i, o,* may follow the tonic syllable. The language, therefore, has a cadence that affects the ear differently from the French, and that resembles more that of the Italian or Spanish languages.

The nasal vowels are again unlike those of the French language. The vowel affected by the following nasal consonant preserves its own quality of sound, and the consonant is pronounced; at the end of a word both *m* and *n* are pronounced as *ng* in the English word *ring*. The Provençal utterance of *matin, tèms,* is therefore quite unlike that of the French *matin, temps.* This change of the nasal consonants into the *ng* sound whenever they become final occurs also in the dialects of northern Italy and northern Spain. This pronunciation of the nasal vowels in French is, as is well known, an important factor in the famous "accent du Midi."

The oral vowels are in general like the French. It is curious that the close *o* is heard only in the infrequent diphthong *óu,* or as an obscured, unaccented final. This absence of the close *o* in the modern language has led Mistral to believe that the close *o* of Old Provençal was pronounced like *ou* in the modern dialect, which regularly represents it. A second element of the "accent du Midi" just referred to is the substitution of an open for a close *o.* The vowel sound of the word *peur* is not distinguished from the close sound in *peu.* In the orthography of the Félibres the diagraph *ue* is used as we find it in Old French to represent this vowel. Probably the most striking feature of the pronunciation is the unusual number of diphthongs and triphthongs, both ascending and descending. Each vowel preserves its proper sound, and the component vowels seem to be pronounced more slowly and separately than in many languages. It is to be noted that *u* in a diphthong has the Italian sound, whereas when single it sounds as in French. The unmarked *e* represents the French *é,* as the *e* mute is unknown to the Provençal.

The *c* has come to sound like *s* before *e* and *i,* as in French. *Ch* and *j* represent the sounds *ts* and *dz* respectively, and *g* before *e* and *i* has the latter sound. There is no aspirate *h.* The *r* is generally uvular. The *s* between vowels is voiced. Only *l, r, s,* and *n* are pronounced as final consonants, *l* being extremely rare. Mistral has preserved or restored other final consonants in order to show the etymology, but they are silent except in *liaison* in the elevated style of reading.

The language is richer in vowel variety than Italian or Spanish, and the proportion of vowel to consonant probably greater than in either. Fortunately for the student, the spelling represents the pronunciation very faithfully. A final consonant preceded by another is mute; among single final consonants only *l, m, n, r, s* are sounded; otherwise all the letters written are pronounced. The stressed syllable is indicated, when not normal, by the application of practically the same principles that determine the marking of the accent in Spanish.

The pronunciation of the Félibres is heard among the people at Maillane and round about. Variations begin as near as Avignon.[5]

Koschwitz' Grammar treats the language historically, and renders unnecessary here the presentation of more than its most striking peculiarities. Of these, one that evokes surprise upon first acquaintance with the dialect is the fact that final *o* marks the feminine of nouns, adjectives, and participles. It is a close *o*, somewhat weakly and obscurely pronounced, as compared, for instance, with the final *o* in Italian. In this respect Provençal is quite anomalous among Romance languages. In some regions of the Alps, at Nice, at Montpellier, at Le Velay, in Haute-Auvergne, in Roussillon, and in Catalonia the Latin final *a* is preserved, as in Italian and Spanish.

The noun has but one form for the singular and plural. The distinction of plural and singular depends upon the article, or upon the demonstrative or possessive adjective accompanying the noun. In *liaison* adjectives take *s* as a plural sign. So that, for the ear, the Provençal and French languages are quite alike in regard to this matter. The Provençal has not even the formal distinction of the nouns in *al*, which in French make their plural in *aux*. *Cheval* in Provençal is *chivau*, and the plural is like the singular. A curious fact is the use of *uni* or *unis*, the plural of the indefinite article, as a sign of the dual number; and this is its exclusive use.

The subject pronoun, when unemphatic, is not expressed, but understood from the termination of the verb. *Iéu* (je), *tu* (tu), and *éu* (il) are used as disjunctive

[5] The edition of *Mirèio* published by Lemerre in 1886 contains an *Avis sur la prononciation provençale* wherein numerous errors are to be noted. Here the statement is made that *all the letters are pronounced*; that *ch* is pronounced *ts*, as in the Spanish word *muchacho*. The fact about the pronunciation of the *ch* is that it varies in different places, having at Maillane the sound *ts*, at Avignon, for instance, the sound in the English *chin*. It is stated further on that *ferramento, capello, fèbre*, are pronounced exactly like the Italian words *ferramento, capello, febbre*. The truth is that they are each pronounced somewhat differently from the Italian words. Provençal knows nothing of double consonants in pronunciation, and the vowels are not precisely alike in each pair of words.

Later this sentence occurs: "Dans les triphthongues, comme *biais, pièi, vuei, niue*, la voix doit dominer sur la voyelle intermédiaire, tout en faisant sentir les autres." Only the first two of these four words contain a triphthong. *Vuei* is a descending diphthong, the *ue* representing the French *eu*. *Niue* offers the same two vowel sounds inverted, with the stress on the second.

Lastly, the example is given of the name Jéuse. It is spelled without the accent mark, and the reader is led to infer that it is pronounced as though it were a French name. Here the *éu* is a diphthong. The first vowel is the French *é*, the second the Italian *u*. The stress is on the first vowel.

forms, in contrast with the French. The possessive adjective *leur* is represented by *si*; and the reflective *se* is used for the first plural as well as for the third singular and third plural.

The moods and tenses correspond exactly to those of the French, and the famous rule of the past participle is identical with the one that prevails in the sister language.

Aside from the omission of the pronoun subject, and the use of one or two constructions not unknown to French, but not admitted to use in the literary language, the syntax of the Provençal is identical with that of the French. The inversions of poetry may disguise this fact a little, but the lack of individuality in the sentence construction is obvious in prose. Translation of Provençal prose into French prose is practically mere word substitution.

Instances of the constructions just mentioned are the following. The relative object pronoun is often repeated as a personal pronoun, so that the verb has its *object* expressed twice. The French continually offers redundancy of subject or complement, but not with the relative.

> "Estre, iéu, lou marran que tóuti L'estrangisson!
> Estre, iéu, l'estrangié que tóuti LOU fugisson!"

> "Être, moi, le paria, que tous rebutent!
> Être, moi, l'étranger que tout le monde fuit!"

(La Rèino Jano, Act I, Scene III.)

The particle *ti* is added to a verb to make it interrogative.

> E.g. soun-ti? sont-ils? Petrarco ignoro-ti?
>
> èro-ti? était-il? Petrarque ignore-t-il?

This is the regular form of interrogative in the third person. It is, of course, entirely due to the influence of colloquial French.

The French indefinite statement with the pronoun *on* may be represented in Provençal by the third plural of the verb; *on m'a demandé* is translated *m'an demanda*, or *on m'a demanda*.

The negative *ne* is often suppressed, even with the correlative *que*.

The verb *estre* is conjugated with itself, as in Italian.

The Provençal speech is, therefore, not at all what it would have been if it had had an independent literary existence since the days of the Troubadours. The influence of the French has been overwhelming, as is naturally to be expected. A great number of idioms, that seem to be pure gallicisms, are found, in spite of the deliberate effort, referred to above, to eliminate French forms. In *La Rèino Jano*, Act III, Scene IV, we find *Ié vai de nòstis os,—Il y va de nos os*. *Vejan, voyons*, is used as a sort of interjection, as in French. The partitive article is used precisely as in French. We meet the narrative infinitive with *de*. In short, the French reader feels at home in the Provençal sentence; it is the same syntax and, to a great degree, the same rhetoric. Only in the vocabulary does he feel himself in a strange atmosphere.

The strength, the originality, the true *raison d'être* of the Provençal speech resides in its rich vocabulary. It contains a great number of terms denoting objects known exclusively in Provence, for which there is no corresponding term in the sister speech. Many plants have simple, familiar names, for which the French must substitute a name that is either only approximate, or learned and pedantic. Words of every category exist to express usages that are exclusively Provençal.

The study of the modern language confirms the results, as regards etymology, reached by Diez and Fauriel and others, who have busied themselves with the Old Provençal. The great mass of the words are traceable to Latin etyma, as in all Romance dialects a large portion of Germanic words are found. Greek and Arabic words are comparatively numerous. Basque and Celtic have contributed various elements, and, as in French, there is a long list of words the origin of which is undetermined.

The language shares with the other southern Romance languages a fondness for diminutives, augmentatives, and pejoratives, and is far richer than French in terminations of these classes. Long suffixes abound, and the style becomes, in consequence, frequently high-sounding and exaggerated.

One of the most evident sources of new words in the language of Mistral is in its suffixes. Most of these are common to the other Romance languages, and have merely undergone the phonetic changes that obtain in this form of speech. In many instances, however, they differ in meaning and in application from their corresponding forms in the sister languages, and a vast number of words are found the formation of which is peculiar to the language under consideration. These suffixes contribute largely to give the language its external appearance; and while a thorough and scientific study of them cannot be given here, enough will be presented to show some of the special developments of Mistral's language in this direction.

-a.

This suffix marks the infinitive of the first conjugation, and also the past participle. It answers to the French forms in -er and -é. As the first conjugation is a so-called "living" conjugation, it is the termination of many new verbs.

-a, -ado.

-ado is the termination of the feminine of the past participle. This often becomes an abstract feminine noun, answering to the French termination -ée; *armée* in Mistral's language is *armado*. Examples of forms peculiar to Provençal are:

óulivo, *an olive.*
óuliva, *to gather olives.*
óulivado, *olive gathering.*
pié, *foot.*
piado, *footprint.*

-age (masc.).

This suffix is the equivalent of the French -age, and is a suffix of frequent occurrence in forming new words. *Óulivage* is a synonym of *óulivado*, mentioned above. A rather curious word is the adverb arrage, meaning *at random, haphazard.* It appears to represent a Latin adverb, *erratice.*

Mourtau, mourtalo, *mortal,* gives the noun mourtalage, *a massacre.*

-agno (fem.).

An interesting example of the use of this suffix is seen in the word eigagno, *dew,* formed from aigo, *water,* as though there had been a Latin word *aquanea.*

-aio (fem.).

This ending corresponds to the French -aille.

poulo, *a hen.*
poulaio, *a lot of hens, poultry.*

-aire (masc.).

This represents the Latin -ator (*one who*). The corresponding feminine in Mistral's works has always the diminutive form -arello.

toumba, *to fall.*
toumbaire, toumbarello, *one who falls* or *one who fells.*
óuliva, *to gather olives.*
óulivaire, óulivarello, *olive gatherer.*
canta, *to sing.*
cantaire, cantarello, *singer.*
panié, *basket.*
panieraire, *basket maker.*
caligna, *to court.*
calignaire, *suitor.*
paternostriaire, *one who is forever praying.*

Like the corresponding French nouns in -eur, these nouns in -aire, as well as those in -èire, are also used as adjectives.

-aire = -arium.

The suffix sometimes represents the Latin -arium. A curious word is *vejaire,* meaning opinion, manner of seeing, as though there had been a Latin word *videarium.* It sometimes has the form *jaire* or *chaire,* through the loss of the first syllable.

-an, -ano.

This suffix is common in the Romance languages. Fihan, *filial,* seems to be peculiar to the Provençal.

-ànci (fem.).

This is the form corresponding to the French -ance. *Abundance* is in Mistral's dialect *aboundànci.*

-ant, -anto.

This is the termination of the present participle and verbal adjective derived from verbs in -a. These words sometimes have a special meaning, as toumbant, *declivity*.

-ard, -ardo.

Gaiard is Provençal for the French *gaillard*.

-àri.

This represents the Latin -arius. Abouticàri is Provençal for *apothecary*.

-as.

This is an augmentative suffix of very frequent use.

porc, *hog*.
pourcas, *great hog*.
serp, *snake*.
serpatas, *great serpent*.
castèu, *fort*.
castelas, *fortress*.
rouco, *rock*.
roucas, *great rock*.

-asso.

This is a pejorative suffix.

vido, *life*.
vidasso, *wretched life*.

-astre.

In French this suffix has the form -âtre.

óulivastre (Fr. olivâtre), *olive in color*.

-at.

Coustat is in French *côté* (side).

The suffix is often diminutive.

auc, *a gander*.
aucat, *gosling*.
passero, *sparrow*.
passerat, *small sparrow*.

-au, -alo.

This is the form of the widely used suffix -al. Mistral uses paternau for *paternal*, and also the adjective formed upon paire, *father*, peirenau, peirenalo, *fatherly*.

bourg, *city*.
bourgau, bourgalo, *civil*.

-edo (fem.).

pin, *pine*.
pinedo, *pine-grove*.
clapo, *stone*.
claparedo, *stony plain*.
óulivo, *olive*.
óulivaredo, *olive-orchard*.

-èire, -erello.

This suffix corresponds to the suffix -aire, mentioned above. It is appended to the stem of verbs not of the first conjugation.

courre, *to run*.
courrèire, courerello, *runner*.
legi, *to read*.
legèire, legerello, *reader*.

-eja.

This is an exceedingly common verb-suffix, corresponding to the Italian -egg-iare.

toumbarèu, *kind of cart*.
toumbaraleja, *to cart*.
farandolo, *farandole*.
farandouleja, *to dance the farandole*.
poutoun, *kiss*.
poutouneja, *to kiss*.
poumpoun, *caress*.
poumpouneja, *to caress*.
segnour, *lord*.
segnoureja, *to lord it over*.
mistral, *wind of the Rhone valley*.
mistraleja, *to roar like the mistral*.
poudro, *powder*.
poudreja, *to fire a gun*.
clar, *bright*.
clareja, *to brighten*.

-en (masc.), -enco (fem.).

This is a common adjective-suffix.

souleu, *sun*.
souleien, souleienco, *sunny*.
mai, *May*.

maien, maienco, *relating to May.*
Madaleno, *Magdalen.*
madalenen, madalenenco, *like Magdalen.*

-ès (masc.), -esso (fem.).

This suffix corresponds to the French -ais, -aise. Liounès = lyonnais.

-et (masc.), -eto (fem.).

This is perhaps the commonest of the diminutive suffixes.

ome, *man.*
oumenet, *little man.*
fiho, *daughter.*
fiheto, *dear daughter.*
enfan, *child.*
enfantounet, *little child.*
vènt, *wind.*
ventoulet, *breeze.*
toumba, *to fall.*
toumbaraleto, *little leaps.*
chato, *girl.*
chatouneto, *little girl*
malaut, *ill.*
malautounet, *sickly.*

It will be observed that the double diminutive termination is the most frequent.

Sometimes the -et is not diminutive. *Óuliveto* may mean a small olive or a field planted with olives.

-èu (masc.), -ello (fem.).

This suffix is often diminutive.

paurin, *poor chap.*
paurinèu paurinello, *poor little fellow or girl.*
pin, *pine.*
pinatèu, *young pine.*
pinatello, *forest of young pines.*
sauvage, *wild.*
sauvagèu, sauvagello, *somewhat wild.*

Sometimes it is not.

toumba, *to fall.*
toumbarèu, -ello, *likely to fall.*
canta, *to sing.*
cantarèu, -ello, *songful.*
crese, *to believe.*

creserèu, -ello, *inclined to belief.*

-i.

This is a verb-suffix, marking the infinitive of a "living" conjugation.

bourgau, *civil.*
abourgali, *to civilize.*

-ié (fem.).

Carestié, *dearness,* stands in contrast to the Italian carestia.

priva, *to train, to tame.*
privadié, *sweet food given in training animals.*

-ié (masc.), -iero (fem.).

This is the equivalent of the French -ier.

óulivié, *olive tree.*
bouchié, *butcher.*
pinatié, } *a dwelling*
pinatiero,} *among pines.*

-ièu (masc.), -ivo (fem.).

This is the form corresponding to the French -if, -ive.

ablatièu, *ablative.*
vièu, vivo, *lively.*

-ige (m.).

According to Mistral, this represents the Latin -ities. We incline to think rather that it corresponds to -age, being added chiefly to words in *e.* -age fits rather upon stems in *a.*

gounfle, *swollen.*
gounflige, *swelling.*
Felibre.
Felibrige.
paure, *poor.*
paurige, *poverty.*

-iho (fem.).

This suffix makes collective nouns.

pastre, *shepherd.*
pastriho, *company of shepherds.*
paure, *poor.*
pauriho, *the poor.*

-in (m.), -ino (fem.).

This is usually diminutive or pejorative.

> paurin, *poor wretch.*

-ioun (fem.).

This corresponds to the French -ion.

> nacioun, *nation.*
> abdicacioun, *abdication.*
> erme, *desert.*
> asserma, *to dry up.*
> assermacioun, *thirst, dryness.*

> -is (masc.), -isso (fem.).

> Crida, *to cry.*
> cridadisso, *cries of woe.*
> chapla, *to slay.*
> chapladis, *slaughter.*
> coula, *to flow.*
> couladis or couladisso, *flowing.*
> abareja, *to throw pell-mell.*
> abarejadis, *confusion.*
> toumba, *to fall.*
> toumbadis, -isso, *tottering* (adj.).

This suffix is added to the past participle stem.

-isoun (fem.).

This suffix forms nouns from verbs in -i.

> abalauvi, *to make dizzy, to confound.*
> abalauvisoun, *vertigo.*

-men (masc.).

This corresponds to the French -ment; bastimen = bâtiment, *ship.*

> abouli, *to abolish.*
> aboulimen, *abolition.*
> toumba, *to fall.*
> toumbamen, *fall.*

-men (adverb).

> urous, urouso, *happy.*
> urousamen, *happily.*

It is to be noted here that the adverb has the vowel of the old feminine termination *a,* and not the modern *o.*

-ot (masc.), -oto (fem.).

A diminutive suffix.

> vilo, *town.*
> viloto, *little town.*

Sometimes the stem no longer exists separately.

> mignot, mignoto, *darling.*
> pichot, pichoto, *little boy, little girl.*

-oto (fem.).

> passa, *to pass.*
> passaroto, *passing to and fro.*

-ou (masc.).

This is a noun-suffix of very frequent use. It seems to be for Latin -or and -orium.

> jouga, *to play.*
> jougadou, *player.*
> abla, *to brag* (cf. Fr. *hâbler*).
> abladou, *braggart.*
> abausi, *to abuse, to exaggerate.*
> abausidou, *braggart.*
> courre, *to run.*
> courredou, *corridor.*
> lava, *to wash.*
> lavadou, *lavatory.*
> espande, *to expand.*
> espandidou, *expanse, panorama.*
> escourre, *to flow out.*
> escourredou, *passage, hollow.*
> toumba, *to fall.*
> toumbadou, *water-fall.*
> abeura, *to water.*
> abeuradou, *drinking-trough.*
> passa, *to sift.*
> passadou, *sieve.*
> mounda, *to winnow.*
> moundadou, *sieve.*

-ouge.

This is an adjective suffix.

> iver, *winter.*
> ivernouge, *wintry.*

-oun (masc.), -ouno (fem.).

A diminutive suffix.

> enfan, *child*.
> enfantoun, enfantouno, *little child*.
> pauriho, *the poor*.
> paurihoun, *poor wretch*.

-ounge (masc.).

A suffix forming nouns from adjectives.

> vièi, *old*.
> vieiounge, *old age*.

-our (fem.).

This is like the above.

> vièi, *old*.
> vièiour, *old age*.

-ous, -ouso.

This is the Latin -osus; French -eux, -euse. It forms many new words in Mistral.

> urous (Fr. heureux), *happy*.
> pouderous (It. and Sp. poderoso), *powerful*.
> aboundous, *abundant*.
> pin, *pine*.
> pinous, *covered with pines*.
> escalabra, *to climb*.
> escalabrous, *precipitous*.

-ta (fem.).

This is the equivalent of the Latin -tas, French -té. In Mistral's language it is usually preceded by a connecting vowel *e*.

> moundaneta, *worldliness*.
> soucieta, *society*.
> paureta, *poverty*.

-u (masc.), -udo (fem.).

This ending terminates the past participles of verbs whose infinitive ends in *e*. It also forms many new adjectives.

> astre, *star*.
> malastru, *ill-starred*.
> sabé, *to know*.
> saberu, *learned*.

The feminine form often becomes a noun.

escourre, *to run out.*
escourregudo, *excursion.*

-un (masc.).

This is a very common noun-suffix.

clar, *bright.*
clarun, *brightness.*
rat, *rat.*
ratun, *lot of rats, smell of rats.*
paure, *poor.*
paurun, *poverty.*
dansa, *to dance.*
dansun, *love of dancing.*
plagne, *to pity.*
plagnun, *complaining.*
vièi, *old.*
vieiun, *old age.*

-uro (fem.).

toumba, *to fall.*
toumbaduro, *a fall.*
escourre, *to flow away.*
escourreduro, *what flows away.*
bagna, *to wet.*
bagnaduro, *dew.*

This partial survey of the subject of the suffixes in Mistral's dialect will suffice to show that it is possible to create words indefinitely. There is no academy to check abuse, no large, cultivated public to disapprove of the new forms. The Félibres have been free. A fondness for diminutives marks all the languages of southern Europe, and a love of long terminations generally distinguished Spanish latinity. The language of the Félibres is by no means free from the grandiloquence and pomposity that results from the employment of these high-sounding and long terminations. *Toumbarelado, toumbarelaire,* are rather big in the majesty of their five syllables to denote a cart-load and its driver respectively. The abundance of this vocabulary is at any rate manifest. We have here not a poor dialect, but one that began with a large vocabulary and in possession of the power of indefinite development and recreation out of its own resources. It forms compounds with greater readiness than French, and the learner is impressed by the unusual number of compound adverbs, some of very peculiar formation. *Tourna-mai* (again) is an example. Somewhat on the model of the French *va-et-vient* is the word *li mounto-davalo,* the ups and downs. *Un regardo-veni* means a look-out. *Noun-ren* is nothingness. *Ped-terrous* (earthy foot) indicates a peasant.

Onomatopoetic words, like *zounzoun, vounvoun, dindánti,* are common.

Very interesting as throwing light upon the Provençal temperament are the numerous and constantly recurring interjections. This trait in the man of the *Midi* is one that Daudet has brought out humorously in the Tartarin books. It is often difficult in serious situations to take these explosive monosyllables seriously.

In his study of Mistral's poetry, Gaston Paris calls attention to the fact that the Provençal vocabulary offers many words of low association, or at least that these words suggest what is low or trivial to the French reader; he admits that the effect upon the Provençal reader may not be, and is likely not to be, the same; but even the latter must occasionally experience a feeling of surprise or slight shock to find such words used in elevated style. For the English reader it is even worse. Many such expressions could not be rendered literally at all. Mistral resents this criticism, and maintains that the words in question are employed in current usage without calling up the image of the low association. This statement, of course, must be accepted. It is true of all languages that words rise and fall in dignity, and their origin and association are momentarily or permanently forgotten.

The undeniably great success of this new Provençal literature justifies completely the revival of the dialect. As Burns speaks from his soul only in the speech of his mother's fireside, so the Provençal nature can only be fully expressed in the home-dialect. Roumanille wrote for Provençals only. Mistral and his associates early became more ambitious. His works have been invariably published with French translations, and more readers know them through the translations than through the originals. But they are what they are because they were conceived in the patois, and because their author was fired with a love of the language itself.

As to the future of this rich and beautiful idiom, nothing can be predicted. The Félibrige movement appears to have endowed southern France with a literary language rivalling the French; it appears to have given an impulse toward the unification of the dialects and subdialects of the *langue d'oc*. But the *patoisants* are numerous and powerful, and will not abdicate their right to continue to speak and write their local dialects in the face of the superiority of the Félibrige literature. Is it to be expected that Frenchmen in the south will hereafter know and use three languages and three literatures—the local dialect, the language of the Félibres, and the national language and literature? One is inclined to think not. The practical difficulties are very great; two literatures are more than most men can become familiar with.

However, this much is certain: a rich, harmonious language has been saved forever and crystallized in works of great beauty; its revival has infused a fresh, intellectual activity into the people whose birthright it is; it has been studied with delight by many who were not born in sunny Provence; a very great contribution is made through it to philological study. Enthusiasts have dreamed of its becoming an international language, on account of its intermediary position, its simplicity, and the fact that it is not the language of any nation. Enthusiasm has here run pretty high, as is apt to be the case in the south.

In connection with the revival of all these dialects the opinion of two men, eminent in the science of education, is of the greatest interest. Eugène Lintilhac approves the view of a professor of Latin, member of the Institute, who had often noticed the superiority of the peasants of the frontier regions over those from the interior, and who said, "It is not surprising, do they not pass their lives translating?" Michel Bréal considers the patois a great help in the study of the official language, on the principle that a term of comparison is necessary in the study of a language. As between Provençal and French this comparison would be between words, rather than in syntax. Often the child's respect for his home would be increased if he sees the antiquity of the speech of his fireside; if, as Bréal puts it, he is shown that his dialect conforms frequently to the speech of Henri IV or St. Louis. "If the province has authors like Jasmin, Roumanille, or Mistral, let the child read their books from time to time along with his French books; he will feel proud of his province, and will love France only the more. The clergy is well aware of this power of the native dialect, and knows how to turn it to account, and your culture is often without root and without depth, because you have not recognized the strength of these bonds that bind to a locality. The school must be fast to the soil and not merely seem to be standing upon it. There need be no fear of thereby shaking the authority of the official language; the necessity of the latter is continually kept in sight by literature, journalism, the administration of government."

The revival of this speech could not fail to interest lovers of literature. If not a lineal descendant, it is at least a descendant, of the language that centuries ago brought an era of beauty and light to Europe, that inspired Dante and Petrarch, and gave to modern literatures the poetic forms that still bear their Provençal names. The modern dialect is devoted to other uses now; it is still a language of brightness and sunshine, graceful and artistic, but instead of giving expression to the conventionalities of courtly love, or tending to soften the natures of fierce feudal barons, it now sings chiefly of the simple, genuine sentiments of the human heart, of the real beauties of nature, of the charm of wholesome, outdoor life, of healthy toil and simple living, of the love of home and country, and brings at least a message of hope and cheer at a time when greater literatures are burdened with a weight of discouragement and pessimism.

CHAPTER IV
THE VERSIFICATION OF THE FÉLIBRES

The versification of the Félibres follows in the main the rules observed by the French poets. As in all the Romance languages the verse consists of a given number of syllables, and the number of stressed syllables in the line is not constant. The few differences to be noted between French verse and Provençal verse arise from three differences in the languages. The Provençal has no *e mute*, and therefore all the syllables theoretically counted are distinctly heard, and the masculine and the feminine rhymes are fully distinguished in pronunciation. The new language possesses a number of diphthongs, and the unaccented part of the diphthong, a *u* or an *i*, constitutes a consonant either before or after a vowel in another word, being really a *w* or a *y*. This prevents hiatus, which is banished from Provençal verse as it is from French, and here again theory and practice are in accord, for the elision of the *e mute* where this *e* follows a vowel readmits hiatus into the French line, and no such phenomenon is known to the Provençal. Thirdly, the stressed syllable of each word is strongly marked, and verse exists as strongly and regularly accentual as in English or German. This is seen in the numerous poems written to be sung to an air already existing. The accents in these pieces fall with the rhythmic beat the English ear is accustomed to and which it so misses on first acquaintance with French verse. A second consequence of this stronger stress is that verse is written without rhyme; the entire *Poem of the Rhone* is written in ten-syllable feminine verses unrhymed.

> "O tèms di vièi d'antico bounoumío,
> Que lis oustau avien ges de sarraio
> E que li gènt, à Coundriéu coume au nostre,
> Se gatihavon, au calèu pèr rire!"

(Canto I.)

Mistral has made use of all the varieties of verse known to the French poets. One of the poems in the *Isclo d'Or* offers an example of fourteen-syllable verse; it is called *L'Amiradou* (The Belvedere). Here are the first two stanzas: —

> "Au castèu de Tarascoun, i'a 'no rèino, i'a 'no fado
> Au castèu de Tarascoun
> I'a 'no fado que s'escound.

> "Aquéu que ié durbira la presoun ounte es clavado
> Aquéu que ié durbira

Belèu elo l'amara."[6]

We may note here instances of the special features of Provençal versification mentioned above. The *i* in *i'a*, the equivalent of the French *il y a*, is really a consonant. This *i* occurs again in the fourth of the lines quoted, so that there is no hiatus between *que* and *ié*. In like manner the *u* of *belèu*, in the last line, stands with the sound of the English *w* between this and *elo*. The *e* of *ounte* is elided. It will be observed that there is a cæsura between the seventh and eighth syllables of the long line, and that the verse has a marked rhythmic beat, with decided trochaic movement, —

$$\acute{\;}\smile\acute{\;}\smile\acute{\;}\smile\acute{\;}\mid\acute{\;}\smile\acute{\;}\smile\acute{\;}\smile\acute{\;}\smile$$

In his use of French Alexandrine, or twelve-syllable verse, Mistral takes few liberties as to cæsura. No ternary verses are found in *Mirèio*, that is, verses that fall into three equal parts. In general, it may be said that his Alexandrines, except in the play *La Rèino Jano*, represent the classical type of the French poets. To be noted, however, is the presence of feminine cæsuras. These occur, not theoretically or intentionally, but as a consequence of pronunciation, and are an additional beauty in that they vary the movement of the lines. The unstressed vowel at the hemistich, theoretically elided, is pronounced because of the natural pause intervening between the two parts of the verse.

"Per óuliva tant d'aubre! — Hòu, tout acò se fai!"

(Mirèio, Canto I.)

In one of the divisions of *Lou Tambour d'Arcolo* (The Drummer of Arcole), the poet uses ten-syllable verse with the cæsura after the sixth syllable, an exceedingly unusual cæsura, imitated from the poem *Girard de Roussillon*.

"Ah! lou pichot tambour | devenguè flòri!
Davans touto l'arma | — do en plen soulèu,
Pèr estelà soun front | d'un rai de glòri," etc.

Elsewhere he uses this verse divided after the fourth syllable, and less frequently after the fifth.

The stanza used by Mistral throughout *Mirèio* and *Calendau* is his own invention. Here is the first stanza of the second canto of *Mirèio*: —

"Cantas, cantas, magnanarello,
Que la culido es cantarello!
Galant soun li magnan e s'endormon di tres:
Lis amourié soun plen de fiho
Que lou bèu tèms escarrabiho,

---

[6] In the castle at Tarascon there is a queen, there is a fairy,
In the castle of Tarascon
There is a fairy in hiding.

The one who shall open the prison wherein she is confined,
The one who shall open for her,
Perhaps she will love him.

> Coume un vòu de blóundis abiho
> Que raubon sa melico i roumanin dóu gres."

This certainly is a stanza of great beauty, and eminently adapted to the language. Mistral is exceedingly skilful in the use of it, distributing pauses effectively, breaking the monotony of the repeated feminine verses with enjambements, and continuing the sense from one stanza to the next. This stanza, like the language, is pretty and would scarcely be a suitable vehicle for poetic expression requiring great depth or stateliness. Provençal verse in general cannot be said to possess majesty or the rich *orchestral* quality Brunetière finds in Victor Hugo. Its qualities are sweetness, daintiness, rapidity, grace, a merry, tripping flow, great smoothness, and very musical rhythm.

Mirèio contains one ballad and two lyrics in a measure differing from that of the rest of the poem. The ballad of the *Bailiff Suffren* has the swing and movement a sea ballad should possess. The stanza is of six lines, of ten syllables each, with the cæsura after the fifth syllable, the rhymes being *abb, aba*.

> "Lou Baile Sufrèn | que sus mar coumando."

In the third canto occurs the famous song *Magali*, so popular in Provence. The melody is printed at the end of the volume. Mirèio's prayer in the tenth canto is in five-syllable verse with rhymes *abbab*.

The poems of the *Isclo d'Or* offer over eighty varieties of strophe, a most remarkable number. This variety is produced by combining in different manners the verse lengths, and by changes in the succession of rhymes. Whatever ingenuity Mistral has exercised in the creation of rhythms, the impression must not be created that inspiration has suffered through attention to mechanism, or that he is to be classed with the old Provençal versifiers or those who flourished in northern France just before the time of Marot. Artifice is always strictly subordinated, and the poet seems to sing spontaneously. No violence is ever done to the language in order to force it into artificial moulds, there is no punning in rhymes, there is nothing that can be charged against the poet as beneath the real dignity of his art.

Let us look at some of the more striking of these verse forms. The second of *Li Cansoun, Lou Bastimen*, offers the following form:—

> "Lou bastimen vèn de Maiorco
> Emé d'arange un cargamen:
> An courouna de vèrdi torco
> L'aubre-mestre dón bastimen:
> Urousamen
> Vèn de Maiorco
> Lou bastimen."[7]

This stanza reproduces in the sixth line the last word of the first, and in the seventh the last word of the fourth.

An excellent example of accentual verse set to an already existing melody is

[7] The ship comes from Majorca with a cargo of oranges: the mainmast of the ship has been crowned with green garlands: safely the ship arrives from Majorca.

seen in *Li Bon Prouvençau*. The air is:—

> "Si le roi m'avait donné
> Paris, sa grand ville."

We quote the first stanza:—

> "Boufo, au siècle mounte sian
> Uno auro superbo
> Que vòu faire rèn qu'un tian
> De tóuti lis erbo:
> Nautri, li bon Prouvençau
> Aparan lou vièi casau
> Ounte fan l'aleto
> Nòsti dindouleto."[8]

This poem scans itself with perfect regularity, and the rhythm of the tune is evident to the reader who may never have heard the actual music.

The stanza of *La Tourre de Barbentano* is as follows:—

> "L'Evesque d'Avignoun, Mounsen Grimau,
> A fa basti 'no tourre à Barbentano
> Qu' enràbio vènt de mar e tremountano
> E fai despoutenta l'Esprit dóu mau.
> Assegurado
> Sus lou roucas
> Forto e carrado
> Escounjurado
> Porto au soulèu soun front bouscas:
> Mememen i fenestro, dins lou cas
> Que vouguèsse lou Diable intra di vitro,
> A fa Mounsen Grimau grava sa mitro."[9]

Here is a stanza of *Lou Renegat*:—

> "Jan de Gounfaroun, pres pèr de coursàri,
> Dins li Janissàri
> Sèt an a servi:
> Fau, encò di Turc, avé la coudeno
> Facho à la cadeno
> Emai au rouvi."[10]

---

[8] There blows, in this age, a proud wind, which would make a mere hash of all herbs: we, the good Provençals, defend the old home over which our swallows hover.

[9] The bishop of Avignon, Monseigneur Grimoard, hath built a tower at Barbentane, which excites the rage of the sea wind and the northern blast, and strips the Spirit of Evil of his power. Solid upon the rock, strong, square, freed of demons, it lifts its fierce brow sunward; likewise upon the windows, in case the devil might wish to enter thereby, Monseigneur Grimoard has had his mitre carved.

[10] John of Gonfaron, captured by corsairs in the Janissaries, served seven years. Among the Turks a man must use his skin to chains and rust.

The stanza employed in *La Cadéno de Moustié* is remarkable in having only one masculine and one feminine rhyme in its seven lines:—

> "Presounié di Sarrasin,
> Engimbra coume un caraco,
> Em' un calot cremesin
> Que lou blanc soulèu eidraco,
> En virant la pouso-raco,
> Rico-raco,
>
> Blacasset pregavo ansin."[11]

The "roumanso" of *La Rèino Jano* offers a stanza containing only five rhymes in fourteen lines:—

> "Fiéu de Maiano
> S'ère vengu dóu tèms
> De Dono Jano,
> Quand èro à soun printèms
> E soubeirano
> Coume èron autre-tèms,
> Sènso autro engano
> Que soun regard courous,
> Auriéu, d'elo amourous,
> Trouva, iéu benurous,
> Tant fino cansouneto
> Que la bello Janeto
> M'aurié douna 'n mantèu
>
> Pèr parèisse i castèu."[12]

The rhythm of the noble *Saume de la Penitènci* is as follows:—

> "Segnour, à la fin ta coulèro
> Largo si tron
> Sus nosti front:
> E dins la niue nosto galèro
> Pico d'a pro
> Contro li ro."[13]

Another peculiar stanza is exhibited in *Lou Prègo-Diéu*:—

> "Ero un tantost d'aquest estiéu
> Que ni vihave ni dourmiéu:
> Fasiéu miejour, tan que me plaise,
> Lou cabassòu

[11] Prisoner of the Saracens, accoutred like a gypsy, with a crimson turban, dried by the white sun, turning the creaking water-wheel, Blac prayed thus.

[12] A son of Maillane, if I had come in the days of Queen Joanna when she was in her springtime and a sovereign such as they were in those days, with no other diplomacy than her bright glance, in love with her, I should have found, lucky I, so fine a song that the fair Joanna would have given me a mantle to appear in the castles.

[13] This poem will be found translated in full at the end of the book.

> Toucant lou sòu,
> A l'aise."[14]

Perhaps the most remarkable of all in point of originality, not to say queerness, is *Lou Blad de Luno*. The rhyme in *lin* is repeated throughout seventeen stanzas, and of course no word is used twice.

> "La luno barbano
> Debano
> De lano.
>
> S'entènd peralin
> L'aigo que lalejo
> E batarelejo
> Darrié lou moulin.
>
> La luno barbano
> Debano
> De lin."[15]

The little poem, *Aubencho*, is interesting as offering two rhymes in its nine lines.

Mistral's sonnets offer some peculiarities. He has one composed of lines of six syllables, others of eight, besides those considered regular in French, consisting, namely, of twelve syllables. The following sonnet addressed to Roumania appears to be unique in form:—

> "Quand lou chaple a pres fin, que lou loup e la rùssi
> An rousiga lis os, lou soulèu flamejant
> Esvalis gaiamen lou brumage destrùssi
> E lou prat bataié tourno lèu verdejant.
>
> "Après lou long trepé di Turc emai di Rùssi
> T'an visto ansin renaisse, o nacioun de Trajan,
> Coume l'astre lusènt, que sort dóu negre eslùssi,
> Emé lou nouvelun di chato de quinge an.
>
> "E li raço latino
> A ta lengo argentino
> An couneigu l'ounour que dins toun sang i'avié;
>
> "E t'apelant germano,
> La Prouvenço roumano
> Te mando, o Roumanio, un rampau d'óulivié."[16]

---

[14] It was an afternoon of this summer,
While I neither woke nor slept,
I was taking my noonday rest, as is my pleasure,
My head touching the ground at ease.

[15] The ghostly moon is unwinding wool.
Afar off is heard the gurgling water shaking the clapper behind the mill.
The ghostly moon is unwinding flax.

[16] When the slaughter is over, when the wolf and the buzzard have gnawed the bones, the flaming sun scatters merrily the hurtful vapors and the battlefield soon becomes

It would be a hopeless task for an English translator to attempt versions of these poems that should reproduce the original strophe forms. A few such translations have been made into German, which possesses a much greater wealth of rhyme than English. Let us repeat that it must not be imputed to Mistral as a fault that he is too clever a versifier. His strophes are not the artificial complications of the Troubadours, and if these greatly varied forms cost him effort to produce, his art is most marvellously concealed. More likely it is that the almost inexhaustible abundance of rhymes in the Provençal, and the ease of construction of merely syllabic verse, explain in great measure his fertility in the production of stanzas. Some others of the Félibres, even Aubanel, in our opinion, have produced verse that is very ordinary in quality. Verse may be made too easily in this dialect, and fluent rhymed language that merely expresses commonplace sentiment may readily be mistaken for poetry.

The wealth of rhyme in the Provençal language appears to be greater than in any other form of Romance speech. As compared with Italian and Spanish, it may be noted that the Provençal has no proparoxytone words, and hence a whole class of words is brought into the two categories possible in Provençal. Though the number of different vowels and diphthongs is greater than in these two languages, only three consonants are found as finals, n, r, s (l very rarely). The consequent great abundance of rhymes is limited by an insistence upon the rich rhyme to an extent scarcely attainable in French; in fact, the merely sufficient rhyme is very rare. It is unfortunate that so many of the feminine rhymes terminate in o. In the *Poem of the Rhone*, composed entirely in feminine verses, passages occur where nine successive lines end in this letter, and the verses in o vastly out-number all others. In this unrhymed poem, assonance is very carefully avoided.

The play, *Queen Joanna*, is remarkable among the productions of Mistral as being the only work of any length he has produced that makes extensive use of the Alexandrine. In fact, the versification is precisely that of any modern French play written in verse; and we may note here the liberties as to cæsura and enjambements which are now usual in French verse. We remark elsewhere the lack of independence in the dialect of Avignon, that its vocabulary alone gives it life. Not only has it no syntax of its own, but it really has been a difficulty of the poet in translating his own Alexandrines into French prose, not to produce verses; nor has he always avoided them. Here, for instance, is a distich which not only becomes French when translated word for word, but also reproduces exactly metre and rhyme:—

> "En un mot tout me dis que lou cèu predestino
> Un reviéure de glòri à terro latino.

> "En un mot tout me dit que le ciel préstine

green once more.

After the long trampling of the Turks and Russians, thou, too, art seen thus reborn, O nation of Trajan, like the shining star coming forth from the dark eclipse, with the youth of a maiden of fifteen.

And the Latin races, in thy silvery speech, have recognized the honor that lay in thy blood; and calling thee sister, the Romance Provence sends thee, Roumania, an olive branch.

Un renouveau de gloire à terre latine."

The effectiveness, the charm, and the beauty of this verse, for those who understand and feel the language, cannot be denied; and if this poetic literature did not meet a want, it could not exist and grow as it does. The fact that the prose literature is so slight, so scanty, is highly significant. The poetry that goes straight to the heart, that speaks to the inner feeling, that calls forth a response, must be composed in the home speech. It is exceedingly unlikely that a prose literature of any importance will ever grow up in Provence. No great historians or dramatists, and few novelists, will ever write in this dialect. The people of Provence will acquire their knowledge and their general higher culture in French literature. But they will doubtless enjoy that poetry best which sings to them of themselves in the speech of their firesides. Mistral has endowed them with a verse language that has high artistic possibilities, some of which he has realized most completely. The music of his verse is the music that expresses the nature of his people. It is the music of the *gai savoir*. Brightness, merriment, movement, quick and sudden emotion,—not often deep or sustained,—exuberance and enthusiasm, love of light and life, are predominant; and the verse, absolutely free from strong and heavy combinations of consonants, ripples and glistens with its pretty terminations, full of color, full of vivacity, full of the sunny south.

CHAPTER V

MISTRAL'S DICTIONARY OF THE PROVENÇAL LANGUAGE. (LOU TRESOR DÓU FÉLIBRIGE)

AU MIEJOUR

Sant Jan, vèngue meissoun, abro si fiò de joio;
Amount sus l'aigo-vers lou pastre pensatiéu,
En l'ounour dóu païs, enausso uno mount-joio
E marco li pasquié mounte a passa l'estiéu.

Emai iéu, en laurant—e quichant moun anchoio,
Per lou noum de Prouvenço ai fa ço que poudiéu;
E, Diéu de moun pres-fa m'aguent douna la voio,
Dins la rego, à geinoui, vuei rènde gràci à Diéu.

En terro, fin qu'au sistre, a cava moun araire;
E lou brounze rouman e l'or dis emperaire
Treluson au soulèu dintre lou blad que sort....

O pople dóu Miejour, escouto moun arengo:
Se vos recounquista l'empèri de ta lengo,
Pèr t'arnesca de nòu, pesco en aquéu Tresor.

"Saint John, at harvest time, kindles his bonfires; high up on the mountain slope the thoughtful shepherd places a pile of stones in honor of the country, and marks the pastures where he has passed the summer.

"I, too, tilling and living frugally, have done what I could for the fame of Provence; and God having permitted me to complete my task, to-day, on my knees in the furrow, I offer thanks to Him.

"My plough has dug into the soil down to the rock; and the Roman bronze and the gold of the emperors gleam in the sunlight among the growing wheat.

"Oh, people of the South, heed my saying: If you wish to win back the empire of your language, equip yourselves anew by drawing upon this Treasury."

Such is the sonnet, dated October 7, 1878, which Mistral has placed at the beginning of his vast dictionary of the dialects of southern France. The title of the work is *Lou Tresor dóu Felibrige* or *Dictionnaire provençal-français*. It is published in two large quarto volumes, offering a total of 2361 pages. This great work occupied the poet some ten years, and is the most complete and most important work of its kind that has been made. The statement that this work represents for the

Provençal dialect what Littré's monumental dictionary is for the French, is not exaggerated. Nothing that Mistral has done entitles him in a greater degree to the gratitude of students of Romance philology, and the fact that the work has been done in so masterful a fashion by one who is not first of all a philologist excites our wonder and admiration. And let us not forget that it was above all else a labor of love, such as probably never was undertaken elsewhere, unless the work of Ivar Aasen in the Old Norse dialects be counted as such; and there is something that appeals strongly to the imagination in the thought of this poet's labor to render imperishable the language so dear to him. Years were spent in journeying about among all classes of people, questioning workmen and sailors, asking them the names they applied to the objects they use, recording their proverbial expressions, noting their peculiarities of pronunciation, listening to the songs of the peasants; and then all was reduced to order and we have a work that is really monumental.

The dictionary professes to contain all the words used in South France, with their meaning in French, their proper and figurative acceptations, augmentatives, diminutives, with examples and quotations. Along with each word we have all its various forms as they appear in the different dialects, its forms in the older dialects, the closely related forms in the other Romance languages, and its etymology. A special feature of the work in view of its destination is the placing of numerous synonyms along with each word. The dictionary almost contains a grammar, for the conjugation of regular and of irregular verbs in all the dialects is given, and each word is treated in its grammatical relations. Technical terms of all arts and trades; popular terms in natural history, with their scientific equivalents; all the geographical names of the region in all their forms; proper historical names; family names common in the south; explanations as to customs, manners, institutions, traditions, and beliefs; biographical, bibliographical, and historical facts of importance; and a complete collection of proverbs, riddles, and popular idioms—such are the contents of this prodigious work.

If any weakness is to be found, it is, of course, in the etymological part. Even here we can but pay tribute to Mistral. If he can be accused, now and then, of suggesting an etymology that is impossible or unscientific, let it be gratefully conceded that his desire is to offer the etymologist all possible help by placing at his disposal all the material that can be found. The pains Mistral has taken to look up all possibly related words in Greek, Arabic, Basque, and English, to say nothing of the Old Provençal and Latin, would alone suffice to call forth the deepest gratitude on the part of all students of the subject.

This dictionary makes order out of chaos, and although the language of the Félibres is justly said to be an artificial literary language, we have in this work along with the form adopted or created by the poet an orderly presentation of all the speech-forms of the *langue d'oc* as they really exist in the mouths of the people.

PART SECOND
THE POETICAL WORKS OF MISTRAL

CHAPTER I

THE FOUR LONGER POEMS

I. MIRÈIO (MIREILLE)

The publication of this poem in 1859 is an event of capital importance in the history of modern Provençal literature. Recognized immediately as a master-work, it fired the ambitions of the Félibres, enlarged the horizon of possibilities for the new speech, and earned for its author the admiration of critics in and out of France. Original in language and in conception, full of the charm of rustic life, containing a pathetic tale of love, a sweet human interest, and glowing with pictures of the strange and lovely landscapes of Provence, the poem charmed all readers, and will doubtless always rank as a work that belongs to general literature. Of no other work written in this dialect can the same be asserted. Mistral has not had an equal success since, and in spite of the merit of his other productions, his literary fame will certainly always be based upon this poem. Whatever be the destiny of this revival, the author of *Mirèio* has probably already taken his place among the immortals of literature.

He has incarnated in this poem all that is sweetest and best, all that is most typical in the life of his region. The tale is told, in general, with complete simplicity, sobriety, and conciseness. The poet's heart and soul are in his work from beginning to end, and it seems more genuinely inspired than any of the long poems he has written subsequently.

In the first canto the author says, —

> "Car cantan que pèr vautre, o pastre e gènt di mas."
> For we sing for you alone, O shepherds and people of the farms,

and when he wrote this verse, he was doubtless sincere. Later, however, he must have become conscious that a work of great artistic beauty was growing under his hand, and that it would find a truly appreciative public more probably among the cultivated classes than among the peasants of Provence. Hence the French prose translation; and hence, furthermore, a paradox in the position Mistral assumed. Since those who really appreciate and admire his poetry are the cultivated classes who know French, and since the peasants who use the dialect cannot feel the artistic worth of his literary production, or even understand the elevated diction he is forced to employ, should he not, after all, have written in French? The idea of Roumanille was simpler and less ambitious than that of Mistral; he aimed to give the humble classes about him a literature within their reach, that should give them moral lessons, and appeal to the best within them. Mistral, developing into a poet of genius while striving to attain the same object, could not fail to change the object, and this contradiction becomes apparent in *Mirèio*, and constitutes a problem in any discussion of his literary work.

The story of *Mirèio* may be told in a few words. She is a beautiful young girl of fifteen, living at the *mas* of her father, Ramoun. She falls in love with a handsome, stalwart youth, Vincèn, son of a poor basket-maker. But the difference in worldly wealth is too great, her father and mother violently oppose their union, and so, one night, the maiden, in despair, rushes away from home, across the great plain of the Crau, across the Rhone, across the island of Camargue, to the church of the three Maries. Vincèn had told her to seek their aid in any time of trouble. Here she prays to the three saints to give Vincèn to her, but the poor girl has been overcome by the terrible heat of the sun in crossing the treeless plains and is found by her parents and friends unconscious before the altar. Vincèn comes also and joins his lamentations to theirs. The holy caskets are lowered from the chapel above, but no prayers avail to save the maiden's life. She expires, with words of hope upon her lips.

This simple tale is told in twelve cantos; it aims to be an epic, and in its external form is such. It employs freely the *merveilleux chrètien*, condemned by Boileau, and in one canto, *La Masco* (The Witch), the poet's desire to embody the superstitions of his ignorant landsmen has led him entirely astray. The opening stanza begins in true epic fashion:—

> "Cante uno chato de Prouvènço
> Dins lis amour de sa jouvènço."

> I sing a maiden of Provence
> In her girlhood's love.

The invocation is addressed to Christ:—

> Thou, Lord God of my native land,
> Who wast born among the shepherd-folk,
> Fire my words and give me breath.

The epic character of the poem is sustained further than in its mere outward form; the manner of telling is truly epic. The art of the poet is throughout singularly objective, his narrative is a narrative of actions, his personages speak and move before us, without intervention on the part of the author to analyze their thoughts and motives. He is absent from his work even in the numerous descriptions. Everything is presented from the outside.

From the outset the poem enjoyed great success, and the enthusiastic praise of Lamartine contributed greatly thereto. In gratitude for this, Mistral dedicated the work to Lamartine in one of his most happy inspirations, and these dedicatory lines appear in *Lis Isclo d'Or* and in all the subsequent editions of *Mirèio*. Mistral had professed great admiration for the author of *Jocelyn* even before 1859, but as poets they stand in marked contrast. We may partly define Mistral's art in stating that it is utterly unlike that of Lamartine. Mistral's inspiration is not that of a Romantic; his art sense is derived directly from the study of the Greek and Roman classics. In all that Mistral has written there is very little that springs from his personal sorrows. The great body of his poetry is epic in character, and the best of his work in the lyric form gives expression not to merely personal emotion, but to the feeling of the race to which he belongs.

The action of the poem begins one day that Vincèn and his father Mèste Ambroi, the basket-makers, were wandering along the road in search of work. Their conversation makes them known, and depicts for us the old *Mas des Micocoules*, the home of the prosperous father of Mirèio. We learn of his wealth in lands, in olives, in almonds, and in bees. We watch the farm-hands coming home at evening. When the basket-makers reach the gate, they find the daughter of the house, who, having just fed her silkworms, is now twisting a skein. The man and the youth ask to sleep for the night upon a haystack, and stop in friendly talk with Mirèio. The poet describes Vincèn, a dark, stalwart youth of sixteen, and tells of his skill at his trade. Mèste Ramoun invites them in to supper. Mirèio runs to serve them. In exquisite verse the poet depicts her grace and beauty.

When all have eaten, at the request of the farm-hands, to which Mirèio adds hers, Mèste Ambroi sings a stirring ballad about the naval victories of Suffren, and the gallant conduct of the Provençal sailors who whipped the British tars.

"And the old basket-maker finished his naval song in time, for his voice was about to break in tears, but too soon, surely, for the farm-hands, for, without moving, with their heads intent and lips parted, *long after the song had ceased, they were listening still.*"

And then the men go about their affairs and leave Vincèn and Mirèio alone together. Their talk is full of charm. Vincèn is eloquent, like a true southerner, and tells his experiences with flashing eye and animated gestures. Here we learn of the belief in the three Maries, who have their church in the Camargue. Here Vincèn narrates a foot-race in which he took part at Nimes, and Mirèio listens in rapt attention.

"It seems to me," said she to her mother, "that for a basket-maker's child he talks wonderfully. O mother, it is a pleasure to sleep in winter, but now the night is too bright to sleep, but let us listen awhile yet. I could pass my evenings and my life listening to him."

The second canto opens with the exquisite stanza beginning, —

"Cantas, cantas, magnanarello
Que la culido es cantarello!"

and the poet evidently fell in love with its music, for he repeats it, with slight variations, several times during the canto. This second canto is a delight from beginning to end; Mistral is here in his element; he is at his very best. The girls sing merrily in the lovely sunshine as they gather the silkworms, Mirèio among them. Vincèn passes along, and the two engage in conversation. Mistral cannot be praised too highly for the sweetness, the naturalness, the animation of this scene. Mirèio learns of Vincèn's lonely winter evenings, of his sister, who is like Mirèio but not so fair, and they forget to work. But they make good the time lost, only now and then their fingers meet as they put the silkworms into the bag. And then they find a nest of little birds, and the saying goes that when two find a nest at the top of a tree a year cannot pass but that Holy Church unite them. So says Mirèio; but Vincèn adds that this is only true if the young escape before they are put into a cage. "Jesu moun Diéu! take care," cries the young girl, "catch them carefully, for this concerns us." So Vincèn gets the young birds, and Mirèio puts them carefully into her bodice; but they dig and scratch, and must be transferred to Vincèn's cap; and then the branch breaks, and the two fall together in close embrace upon the soft grass. The poet breaks into song:—

"Fresh breezes, that stir the canopy of the woods, let your merry murmur soften into silence over the young couple! Wandering zephyrs, breathe softly, give time to dream, give them time at least to dream of happiness! Thou that ripplest o'er thy bed, go slowly, slowly, little brook! Make not so much sound among the stones, make not so much sound, for the two souls have gone off, in the same beam of fire, like a swarming hive—let them hover in the starry air!"

But Mirèio quickly releases herself; the young man is full of anxiety lest she be hurt, and curses the devilish tree "planted a Friday!" But she, with a trembling she cannot control, tells of an inner torment that takes away hearing and sight, and keeps her heart beating. Vincèn wonders if it may not be fear of a scolding from her mother, or a sunstroke. Then Mirèio, in a sudden outburst, like a Wagnerian heroine, confesses her love to the astonished boy, who remains dazed, and believes for a time that she is cruelly trifling with him. She reassures him, passionately. "Do not speak so," cries the boy, "from me to you there is a labyrinth; you are the queen of the Mas, all bow before you; I, peasant of Valabrègue, am nothing, Mirèio, but a worker in the fields!" "Ah, what is it to me whether my beloved be a baron or a basket-weaver, provided he is pleasing to me. Why, O Vincèn, in your rags do you appear to me so handsome?"

And then the young man is as inspired, and in impassioned, well-nigh extravagant language tells of his love for Mirèio. He is like a fig tree he once saw that grew thin and miserable out of a rock near Vaucluse, and once a year the water comes and the tree quenches its thirst, and renews its life for a year. And the youth is the fig tree and Mirèio the fountain. "And would to Heaven, would to Heaven, that I, poor boy, that I might once a year, as now, upon my knees, sun myself in the beams of thy countenance, and graze thy fingers with a trembling kiss." And then her mother calls. Mirèio runs to the house, while he stands motionless as in a dream.

No résumé or even translation can give the beauty of this canto, its brightness, its music, its vivacity, the perfect harmony between words and sense, the graceful succession of the rhymes and the cadence of the stanzas. Elsewhere in the chapter on versification a reference is made to the mechanical difficulties of translation, but there are difficulties of a deeper order. The Félibres put forth great claims for the richness of their vocabulary, and they undoubtedly exaggerate. Yet, how shall we render into English or French the word *embessouna* when describing the fall of Mirèio and Vincèn from the tree. Mistral writes:—

"Toumbon, embessouna, sus lou souple margai."

Bessoun (in French, *besson*) means a twin, and the participle expresses the idea, *clasped together like twins*. (Mistral translates, "serrés comme deux jumeaux.") An expression of this sort, of course, adds little to the prose language; but this power, untrammelled by academic traditions, of creating a word for the moment, is essential to the freshness of poetic style.

What is to be praised above all in these two exquisite cantos is the pervading naturalness. The similes and metaphors, however bold and original, are always drawn from the life of the speakers. Mèste Ambroi, declining at first to sing, says *"Li mirau soun creba!"* (The mirrors are broken), referring to the membranes of the locust that make its song. "Like a scythe under the hammer," "Their heads leaning together like two marsh-flowers in bloom, blowing in the merry wind," "His words flowed abundantly like a sudden shower on an aftermath in May," "When your eyes beam upon me, it seems to me I drink a draught of perfumed wine," "My sister is burned like a branch of the date tree," "You are like the asphodel, and the tanned hand of Summer dares not caress your white brow," "Slender as a dragon-fly," are comparisons taken at random. Of Mirèio the poet says, "The merry sun hath hatched her out," "Her glance is like dew, her rounded bosom is a double peach not yet ripe."

The background of the action is obtained by the simplest description, a cart casting the shadow of its great wheels, a bell now and then sounding afar off across the marshes, references to the owl adding its plaint to the song of the nightingale, to the crickets who stop to listen now and then, and the recurring verses about the "magnanarello" reminds us now and then, like a lovely leitmotiv, of the group of singing girls about the amorous pair.

The next canto is called *La Descoucounado* (The Opening of the Cocoons), and it must be confessed that there is a slight falling off in interest. All that describes the life of the country-folk is full of sustained charm, but Mistral has not escaped the dangers that beset the modern poet who aims at the epic style. Here begins the recounting of the numerous superstitions of the ignorant peasants, and the wonders of Provence are interpolated at every turn. The maidens, while engaged in stripping the cocoons, make known a long list of popular beliefs, and then branch off into a conversation about love. They are surprisingly well acquainted with the writings of Jean de Nostradamus, to whom the Félibres are indebted for a lot of erroneous ideas concerning the Troubadours and the Courts of Love. This literary conversation is not convincing, and we are pleased when Noro sings the pretty song of Magali, which, composed to be sung to an air well known in Provence, has become very popular. The idea is not new; the young girl sings of successive forms she will assume, to avoid the attentions of her suitor, and he, ingeniously, finds the transformation necessary to overcome her. For instance, when she becomes a rose, he changes into a butterfly to kiss her. At last the maiden becomes convinced of the love of her pursuer, and is won.

The fourth canto, *Li Demandaire* (The Suitors), recalls the Homeric style, and is among the finest of the poem. Alàri, the shepherd, Veran, the keeper of horses, and

Ourrias, who has herds of bulls in the Camargue, present themselves successively for the hand of Mirèio. The "transhumance des troupeaux" is described in verse full of vigorous movement; the sheep are taken up into the Alps for the summer, and then in the fall brought down to the great plain of the Crau near the Delta of the Rhone. The whole description is made with bold, simple strokes of the brush, offering a vivid picture not to be forgotten. Alàri, too, offers a marvellously carved wooden cup, adorned with pastoral scenes. Veran owns a hundred white mares, whose manes, thick and flowing like the grass of the marshes, are untouched by the shears, and float above their necks, as they bound fiercely along, like a fairy's scarf. They are never subdued, and often, after years of exile from the salt meadows of the Camargue, they throw off their rider, and gallop over twenty leagues of marshes to the land of their birth, to breathe the free salt air of the sea. Their element is the sea; they have surely broken loose from the chariot of Neptune; they are still white with foam; and when the sea roars and darkens, when the ships break their cables, the stallions of the Camargue neigh with joy.

And Ramoun welcomes Veran, and hopes that Mirèio will wed him, and calls his daughter, who gently refuses. The third suitor, Ourrias, has no better fortune. The account of this man's giant strength, the narrative of his exploits in subduing the wild bulls, are quite Homeric. The story is told of the scar he bears, how one of the fiercest bulls that he had branded carried him along, threw him ahead on the ground, and then hurled him high into the air. The strong, fierce man presents his suit, describing the life the women lead in the Camargue; but before he has her love, "his trident will bear flowers, the hills will melt away like wax, and the journey to Les Baux will be by sea." This canto and the next, recounting the fierce combat between Ourrias and Vincèn, are really splendid narrative poetry. The style is marvellously compressed, and the story thrilling. The sullen anger of Ourrias, his insult that does not spare Mirèio, the indignation of Vincèn, that fires him with unwonted strength, the battle of the two men out alone in the fields near the mighty Pont du Gard, Vincèn's victory in the trial of strength, the treachery of Ourrias, who sneaks back and strikes his enemy down with the trident. "With a mighty groan the hapless boy rolls at full length upon the grass, and the grass yields, bloody, and over his earthy limbs the ants of the fields already make their way." The rapidity, the compactness of the sentences, impressed Gaston Paris as very remarkable. The assassin gallops away upon his mare, and seeks by night to cross the Rhone. A singularly felicitous use of the supernatural is made here. Ourrias is carried to the bottom of the river by the goblins and spirits that come out and hover over it at night. There is a certain terror in this termination, something that recalls parts of the Inferno. Ourrias's superstitious fears are the effect of his guilty conscience. The souls of the damned, their weird ceremonial, are but the outward rendering of the inward terror he feels.

A less legitimate use of the supernatural is made in the succeeding canto, called *La Masco* (The Witch). In fact, the canto is really a blemish in the beautiful poem. Vincèn is found unconscious and carried to the Mas des Micocoules, and various remedies tried. He comes to himself, but the wound is deemed too serious to be healed by natural means, and Mirèio, at the suggestion of one of her maiden friends, takes Vincèn to the abode of the witch who lives in the Fairies' Hole under the rocks of Les Baux. Besides the obvious objection that the magic cure could not have been made, there is the physical impossibility of Vincèn's having walked, in his dying condition, through the labyrinth of subterranean passages, amid the wild scenes of a sort of Walpurgis night. The poet was doubtless led into this error by his desire to preserve all the legends and superstitious lore of Provence. Possibly he was led astray also by his desire to create an epic poem, in which a visit to the lower regions is a necessity. The entire episode is impossible and uninteresting, and is a blot in the beautiful idyll. Later on, this desire to insert the supernatural leads the poet to interrupt the action of his poem, while the three Maries relate to the unconscious Mirèio at great length the story of their coming from Jerusalem to Provence. Interesting as folklore, or as an evidence of the credulity of the Provençals, this narrative of the three Maries is out of place in the poem. It does not help us out to suppose that Mirèio dreams the narrative, for it is full of theology, history, and traditions she could not possibly have conceived. The poem of *Mirèio* and all Mistral's work suffer from this desire to work into his poetry all the history, real and legendary, of his region.

The three Maries are Mary Magdalen, Mary, the mother of James and John, and Mary, the mother of James the Less. After the Crucifixion they embark with Saint Trophime, and successfully battling with the storms of the sea, they land finally in Provence, and by a series of miracles convert the people of Arles. This canto never would have converted Boileau from his disapproval of the "merveilleux chrétien."

The poet finds his true inspiration again in the life of the Mas, in the home-bringing of the crops, in the gathering of the workers about the table of Mèste Ramoun. This picture of patriarchal life is like a bit out of an ancient literature; we have a feeling of the archaic, of the primitive, we are amid the first elements of human life, where none of the complications of the modern man find a place. Mèste Ambroi, whom Vincèn has finally persuaded with passionate entreaties to seek the hand of Mirèio for him, comes upon this evening scene. The interview of the two old men is like a Greek play; their wisdom and experience are uttered in stately, sententious language, and many a proverb falls from their lips. Ramoun has inflexible ideas as to parental authority: "A father is a father, his will must be done. The herd that leads the herdsman, sooner or later, is crunched in the jaws of the wolf. If a son resisted his father in our day, the father would have slain him perhaps! Therefore the families were strong, united, sound, resisting the storm like a line of plane trees! Doubtless they had their quarrels, as we know, but when Christmas night, beneath its starry tent, brought together the head of the house and his descendants, before the blessed table, before the table where he presided, the old man, with his wrinkled hand, washed it all away with his benediction!"

But Mirèio and not Mèste Ambroi makes known to her father that it is her hand Vincèn seeks, and the mother and father break out in anger against the maid. Ramoun's anger leads him to speak offensively to Mèste Ambroi, who nobly maintains his dignity amid his poverty, and recounts his services to his country that have been so ill repaid. Ramoun is equally proud of his wealth, earned by the sweat of his brow, and sternly refuses. The other leaves, and then the harvesters continue their merry-making, with singing and farandoles, about a great bonfire in honor of Saint John. "All the hills were aglow as if stars had rained in the darkness, and the mad wind carried up the incense of the hills and the red gleam of the fires toward the saint, hovering in the blue twilight."

That night Mirèio grieved and wept for Vincèn, and, remembering what he had told her of the three Saint Maries, rises before the dawn and flees away. Her journey across the Crau and the island of Camargue is narrated with numerous details and descriptions; they are never extraneous to the action, and are a constant source of beauty and interest. The strange, barren plain of the Crau, covered with the stones that once destroyed a race of Giants, as the legend has it, is vividly described, as the maiden flies across it in the ardent rays of the June sun. She stops to pray to a saint that he send her a draught of water, and immediately she comes upon a well. Here she meets a little Arlesian boy who tells her "in his golden speech" of the glories of Arles. "But," says the poet, "O soft, dark city, the child forgot to tell thy supreme wonder; O fertile land of Arles, Heaven gives pure beauty to thy daughters, as it gives grapes to the autumn, and perfumes to the mountains and wings to the bird." The little fellow talks of many things and leads her to his home. From here the fisherman ferries her over the broad Rhone, and we accompany her over the Camargue, down to the sea. A mirage deceives her for a time, she sees the town and church, but it soon vanishes in air, and the maiden hurries on in the fierce heat.

Her prayer in the chapel is written in another verse form:—

"O Santi Mario
Que poudès en flour
Chanja nòsti plour
Clinas lèu l'auriho
De-vers ma doulour!"

O Holy Maries, who can change our tears to blossoms, incline quickly an ear unto my grief!

Before the prayer is ended, there begins the vision of the three Maries, descending to her from Heaven.

Mèste Ramoun discovers the flight of the unhappy maiden, and with all his family starts in pursuit. After the first outburst of grief, he sends out a messenger.

"Let the mowers and the ploughmen leave the scythes and the ploughs! Say to the harvesters to throw down their sickles, bid the shepherds leave their flocks, bid them come to me!"

The boy goes out into the fields, among the mowers and gleaners, and everywhere solemnly delivers his message in the selfsame words. He goes down to the Crau, among the dwarf oaks, and summons the shepherds. All these toilers gather about the head of the farm and his wife, who await them in gloomy silence. Mèste Ramoun, without making clear what misfortune has overtaken him, entreats the men to tell him what they have seen. And the chief of the haymakers, father of seven sons, tells of an evil omen, how, for the first time in thirty years, at the beginning of his day's work, he had cut himself. The parents moan the more. Then a mower from Tarascon tells how as he began his work he had discovered a nest wherein the young birds had been done to death by a myriad of invading ants. Again "the tale of woe was a lance-thrust for the father and mother." A third had been taken as with epilepsy, a shudder had passed over him, and through his dishevelled hair as through the heads of thistles he had felt Death pass like a wind. A fourth had seen Mirèio just before the dawn, and had heard her say, "Will none among the shepherds come with me to the Holy Maries?" And then while the mother laments, preparations are made to follow the maiden to the shrines out yonder by the sea.

This poem, then, depicts for us the rustic life of Provence in all its outward aspects. The pretty tale and the description of the life of the Mas and of the Provençal landscapes are inseparably woven together, forming an harmonious whole. It is not a tragedy, all the characters are too utterly lacking in depth. Vincèn and Mirèio are but a boy and a girl, children just awakening to life. The reader may be reminded of Hermann and Dorothea, of Gabriel and Evangeline, but the creations of the German and the American poet are greatly superior in all that represents study of the human mind and heart.

Goethe's poem and Mistral's have several points of likeness. Hermann seeks to marry against his father's wish, and the objection is the poverty of Dorothea. The case is merely inverted. Both poems imitate the Homeric style, Goethe's more palpably than Mistral's, since the German poet has adopted the Homeric verse. He affects, also, certain recurring terms of expression, "Also sprach sie" and the like, and there is a rather artificial seeking after simplicity of expression. Goethe's poem is more interesting because of the greater solidity of the characters, and because of the more closely knitted plot. The curiosity of the reader is kept roused as in a well-constructed romance. Mistral's poem has, after all, scarcely any more real local color; the rustic life of the two poems is similar, allowing for geographical differences, and we carry away quite as real a picture of Hermann's home and the fields about it as of the Mas of Mèste Ramoun. Mistral's idyll terminates tragically in that Mirèio dies of sunstroke, leaving her lover to mourn, but the tenor of the German poem is more serious and moves us more deeply; the background of war contributes to this, but the source of our emotion is in the deep seriousness of the characters themselves.

Vincèn and Mirèio are charming in their naïveté, they are unspoiled and unreflecting. They are children, and lacking in well-defined personality. They have no knowledge of anything beyond the customs and superstitions of the simple folk about them. Their religion, which is so continually before us, furnishing the very mainspring of the fatal dénouement, is of the most superficial sort, if it can be called religion at all. Whether you are bitten by a dog, a wolf, or a snake, or lose your eyesight, or are in danger of losing your lover, you run to the shrine of some saint for help. The religious feeling really runs no deeper. In his outburst of grief upon seeing Mirèio prone upon the floor of the chapel, the unhappy boy asks what he has done to merit such a blow. "Has he lit his pipe in a church at the lamp? or dragged the crucifix among thistles, like the Jews?" Of the deeper, nobler consolations of religion, of the problems of human destiny, of the relations of religious conviction to human conduct, there is no inkling.

All the characters are equally on the surface. They are types rather than individuals. They have in common the gift of eloquence. They have no thought-life, no meditation. They are eminently sociable, frequently loquacious. They make you think of Daudet's statement concerning the man of the south, "When he is not talking, he is not thinking." But they talk well, and have to an eminent degree the gift of narrative. Vincèn's stories of what he knows and has seen are told most beautifully, and the poet never forgets himself by making the boy utter thoughts he could not have conceived. The boy is merely a child of his race. In any rustic gathering in southern France you may hear a man of the people speak dramatically and thrillingly, with resonant voice and vivid gestures, with a marvellous power of mimicry, and the faces of the listeners reflect all the emotions of the speaker. The numerous scenes, therefore, wherein a group of listeners follow with keenest interest a tale that is told, are eminently true to life. The supreme merit of Mirèio lies in this power of narration that its author possesses. It is all action from beginning to end, and even the digressions and episodes, which occasionally arrest the flow of the narrative, are in themselves admirable pieces of narrative. Most critics have found fault with these episodes and the frequent insertion of legends. In defence of the author, it may be said, that he must have feared while writing Mirèio that it might be his last and only opportunity to address his countrymen in their own dialect, and in his desire to bring them back to a love of the traditions of Provence, he yielded to the temptation to crowd his poem rather more than he would otherwise have done.

Mirèio, then, is a lovely poem, an idyll, a charming, vivid picture of life in the rural parts of the Rhone region. It is singularly original. Local color is its very essence. Its thought and action are strictly circumscribed within the boundaries of the Crau and the Camargue, and its originality consists in this limitation, in the fact that a poet of this century has written a work that comes within the definition of an epic, with all the primitive simplicity of Biblical or Classic writers, without any agitation of the problems of modern life, without any new thought or feeling concerning love or death, or man's relation to the universe, using a dialect unknown at the time beyond the region described. Its success could scarcely have been attained without the poet's masterly prose translation, and yet it is evident that the poem could not have been conceived and carried out in French verse. The freshness, the artlessness, the lack of modernity, would have suffered if the poet had bent his inspiration to the official language. Using a new idiom, wherein he practically had no predecessor, he was free to create expression as he went along, and was not compelled to cast his thought in existing moulds.

The poem cannot place its author among the very great poets of the world, if only because of this limitation. It lacks the breadth and depth, the everlasting interest. But it is a work of great beauty, of wonderful purity, a sweet story, told in lovely, limpid language, and will cause many eyes to turn awhile from other lands to the sunny landscapes of southern France.

II. CALENDAU (CALENDAL)

Mistral spent seven years in elaborating his second epic, as he did in writing his first. The poem had not a popular success, and the reason is not far to seek. The most striking limitation of the poet is his failure to create beings of flesh and blood. Even in Mirèio this lack of well-defined individuality in the characters begins to be apparent, but, in general, the action of the earlier poem is confined to the world of realities, whereas in *Calendau* the poet has given free play to a brilliant and vivid imagination, launching forth into the heroic and incredible, yet without abandoning the world of real time and real places. Allegory and symbolism are the web and woof of *Calendau*. The poem, again, is overburdened with minute historic details and descriptions, which are greatly magnified in the eye of his imagination. A poet, of course, must be pardoned for this want of a sense of proportion, but even a Provençal reader cannot be kept in constant illusion as to the greatness of little places that can scarcely be found upon the map, or dazzled by the magnificence of achievements that really have left little or no impress upon the history of the world. As we follow the poet's work in its chronological development, we find this trait growing more and more pronounced. He sees his beloved Provence, its past and present, and its future, too, in a magnifying mirror that embellishes all it reflects with splendid, glowing colors, and exalts little figures to colossal proportions. The reader falls easily under the spell of this exuberant enthusiasm and is charmed by the poetic power evinced. The wealth of words, the beauty of the imagery with which, for example, the humble, well-nigh unknown little port of Cassis and its fishing industry are described, carry us along and hold us in momentary illusion. We see them in the poet's magic mirror for the time. To the traveller or the sober historian all these things appear very, very different.

With the Félibres the success of the poem was much greater; it is a kind of patriotic hymn, a glorification of the past of Provence, and a song of hope for its future. Its allegory, its learned literary allusions, its delving into obscure historic events, preclude any hope of popular success.

Like *Mirèio*, the poem is divided into twelve cantos, and the form of stanza employed is the same. The heroic tone of the poem might be thought to have required verse of greater stateliness; the recurrence of the three feminine rhymes in the shorter verses often seems too pretty. Like *Mirèio*, the poem has the outward marks of an epic. Unlike *Mirèio*, it reminds us frequently of the *Chansons de geste*, and we see that the author has been living in the world of the Old Provençal poets. This is apparent not merely in the constant allusions, in the reproductions of episodes, but in the manner in which the narrative moves along. Lamartine would not have been reminded of the ancient Greek poets had *Calendau* preceded *Mirèio*. The conception of courtly love, the guiding, elevating inspiration of Beatrice, leading Dante on to greater, higher, more spiritual things, are the sources of the chief ideas contained in *Calendau*. Vincèn and Mirèio remain throughout the simple youth and maiden they were, but Calendau, "the simple fisherman of Cassis," develops into a great hero, performing Herculean tasks, like a knight of the days of chivalry, and rises higher and higher until he wins "the empire of pure love" —his lady's hand.

Very beautiful is the invocation addressed to the "soul of his country that ra-diates, manifest in its language and in its history—that through the greatness of its memories saves hope for him." It is the spirit that inspired the sweet Troubadours, and set the voice of Mirabeau thundering like the mistral. The poet proclaims his belief in his race. "For the waves of the ages and their storms and horrors mingle the nations and wipe out frontiers in vain. Mother Earth, Nature, ever feeds her sons with the same milk, her hard breast will ever give the fine oil to the olive; Spirit, ever springing into life, joyous, proud, and living spirit that neighest in the noise of the Rhone and in the wind thereof! spirit of the harmonious woods, and of the sunny bays, pious soul of the fatherland, I call thee! be incarnate in my Provençal verse!"

We are plunged in orthodox fashion *in medias res*. The young fisherman is seated upon the rocky heights above the sea before the beautiful woman he loves. He does not know who she is; he has performed almost superhuman exploits to win her; but there is an obstacle to their union. She relates that she is the last of the family of the Princes des Baux, who had their castle and city hewn out of the solid rock in the strange mountains that overlook the plain of Arles. She tells the marvellous history of the family, evoking a vision of the days of courtly love when the Troubadours sang at the feet of the fair princesses. A panorama of the life of those days of poetry and song moves before us. The princess even describes and defines in poetic language the forms of verse in vogue in the ancient days, the *Tenson*, the *Pastoral*, the *Ballad*, the *Sirventés*, the *Romance*, the *Congé*, the *Aubade*, the *Solace of Love*. She relates her marriage with the Count Sévéran, who fascinated her by some mysterious power. At the wedding-feast she learns that he is a mere bandit, leader of a band of robbers that infests the country. She fled away through the mountains and found the grotto where she now lives. The fishermen, seeing her appear and vanish among the cliffs, take her to be the fairy Esterello, who is a sort of Loreley. Calendau determines that either Sévéran or he shall die, and seeks him out. His splendid physical appearance and bold, defiant manner arouse in the bandit a desire to get Calendau to join his company, and the women of the band are charmed with him. They ask to hear the story of his life, and the great body of the poem consists of the narrative by Calendau of his exploits. After the last one Calendau has risen to the loftiest conception of pure love through the guidance of Esterello, like Dante inspired by Beatrice. Then the Count holds an orgy and tries to tempt the virtue of the hero. Calendau, after witnessing the lascivious dances, challenges the Count to mortal combat. The latter knows now who he is, and that Esterello is none other than the bride who fled after the marriage-feast. Calendau is overpowered and imprisoned, and the Count and his men set off in search of Esterello. But Calendau is freed by Fourtuneto, one of the women, and journeys by sea from Cannes to Cassis to defend the Princess. Here a great combat takes place with the Count, who fires the pine-woods and perishes miserably, uttering blasphemous imprecations. The Cassidians fight the fire, and Calendau and the blond Princess are saved.

"The applause of two thousand souls salutes them and acclaims them. 'Calen-dau, Calendau, let us plant the May for the conqueror of Esterello. He glorifies, he brings to the light our little harbor of fishermen, let us make him Consul, Consul for life!' So saying the multitude accompanies the generous, happy pair of lovers, and the sun that God rules, the great sun, rises, illumines, and procreates endlessly new enthusiasms, new lovers."

The poem clearly symbolizes the Provençal renascence; Calendau typifies the modern Provençal people, rising to an ideal life and great achievements through the memory of their traditions, and this ideal, this memory, are personified in the person of the beautiful Princess.

The time of the action is the eighteenth century, before the Revolution. This is a deliberate choice of the poet who has a temporal symbolism in mind. "I shall thus combine in my picture the three aspects of Provence on the eve of the Revolution: in the background, the noble legends of the past; in the foreground the social corruption of the evil days; and before us the better future, the future and the reparation personified in the son of the working classes, guardians of the tradition of the country."

As regards the execution, it is masterly, and cannot be ranked below *Mirèio*. There is the same enthusiastic love of nature, the same astonishing resources of expression, the same novelty and originality. In place of the rustic nature of Mirèio, we have the wild grandeur of mountains and sea. There is the same, nay, even greater, eloquence of the speakers, the same musical verse.

> "Car, d'aquesto ouro, ounto es la raro
> Que di delice nous separo,
> Jouine, amourous que siam, libre coume d'aucèu?
> Regardo: la Naturo brulo
> A noste entour, e se barrulo
> Dins li bras de l'Estiéu, e chulo
> Lou devourant alen de soun nòve roussèu.

> "Li serre clar e blu, li colo
> Palo de la calour e molo,
> Boulegon trefouli si mourre.... Ve la mar:
> Courouso e lindo coumo un vèire,
> Dòu grand soulèu i rai bevèire
> Enjusqu'au founs se laisso vèire,
> Se laisso coutiga pèr lou Rose e lou Var."

"For now, where is the limit that separates us from joy, young, amorous as we are, free as birds! Look: Nature burns around us and rolls in the arms of Summer, and drinks in the devouring breath of her ruddy spouse. The clear, blue peaks, the hills, pale and soft with the heat, are thrilled and stir their rounding summits. Behold the sea, glistening and limpid as glass; in the thirsty rays of the great sun, she allows herself to be seen clear to the bottom, to be caressed by the Rhone and the Var."

These are the words of Calendau when, seeking his reward after his final exploit, he learns that he has won the love of Esterello. The poet never goes further in the voluptuous strain, and the mere music of the words, especially beginning

"Ve la mar" is exquisite. They are found in the first canto. This scene wherein the Princess refuses to wed Calendau is typical of the poet. The northern temperament is not impressed with these long tirades, full of ejaculations and apostrophes; they are apt to seem unnatural, insincere, and theatrical. Intense feeling is not so verbose in the north. In this particular Mistral is true to his race. We quote entire the words of Calendau after the refusal of Esterello, itself full exclamation and apostrophizing:—

"Then I have but won the thirst, the weariness of the midshipman, when he is about to reach the summit of the mainmast, and sees gleaming at the limit of the liquid plain naught but water, water eternally! Well, if thou wilt hear it, listen! and let the heath resound with it! It is thou, false woman that thou art, it is thou that hast deceived me, luring me on to believe that at the summit of the peaks I should find the splendor of a sublime dawn, that after winter spring would come, that there is nothing so good as the food earned by labor. Thou hast deceived me, for in the wilderness I found naught but drought; and the wind of this world and its idle noise, the embarrassment of luxury, and the din of glory, and what is called the enjoyment of triumph, are not worth a little hour of love beneath a pine tree! See, from my hand the bridle escapes, my skull is bursting, and I am not sure now that the people in their fear are not right in dreading thee like a ghost, now that I feel, as my reward, thy burning poison streaming through my heart. Yes, thou art the fairy Esterello, and thou art unmasked at last, cruel creature! In the chill of thy refusal I have known the viper. Thou art Esterello, bitter foe to man, haunting the wild places, crowned with nettles, defending the desert against those who clear the land. Thou art Esterello, the fairy that sends a shudder through the foliage of the woods and the hair of the terrified hermit; that fires with the desire of her perfumed embrace her suitors and in malevolence drives them to despair with infernal longings.

"My head is bursting, and since from the heights of my supernatural love a thunderbolt thus hurls me down, since, nothing, nothing henceforth, from this moment on, can give me joy, since, cruel woman, when thou couldst throw me a rope, thou leavest me, in dismay, to drink the bitter current—let death come, black hiding-place, bottomless abyss! let me plunge down head first!"

And when Esterello, fearing he will slay himself, clasps him about the neck, they stand silently embraced, "the tears, in tender mingling, rain from their eyes; despair, agitation, a spell of happiness, keep their lips idle, and from hell, at one bound, they rise to paradise."

Like the creations of Victor Hugo's poetry, those of Mistral speak the language of the author. They have his eloquence, his violent energy of figurative speech, his love of the wild, sunny landscapes about them; they thrill as he does, at the memories of the past; they love, as he does, enumerations of trees and plants; they have his fondness for action.

The poem is filled with interesting episodes. One that is very striking in the narrative of Esterello we shall here reproduce.

We are at the wedding feast of Count Séveran and the Princess des Baux. The merry-making begins to be riotous, and the Count has made a speech in honor of his bride, promising to take her after the melting of the snows to his Alpine palaces, where the walls are of steel, the doors of silver, the locks of gold, and when the sun shines their crystal roofs glitter like flame.

"Scarcely from his lips had fallen these wild words, when the door of the banquet hall opens, and we see the head of an old man, wearing a bonnet and a garment of rough cloth; we see the dust and sweat trickling down his tanned cheeks. The bridegroom, with a terrible glance, like the lightning flash of a fearful storm, turns suddenly pale, and seeks to stop him; but he, whom the glance cannot harm, calmly, impassively, like God when he clothes himself like a poor man, to confound sometimes some rich evil-doer, slowly advances toward the bridegroom, crosses his arms, and scans his countenance. And he says not a word to any one, and all are afraid; a weight of lead lies upon every heart, and from without there seems to blow in upon the lamps an icy wind.

"Finally, a few of them, shaking off their oppression, 'If there come not soon a famine to wipe out this hideous tribe, we shall be eaten by beggars within four days! To the merry bridal pair, what hast thou to say, old scullion?' And they continue to taunt him cruelly. The outraged peasant holds his peace. 'With his blear eyes, his white pate, his limping leg, whither comes he trudging? Pelican, bird of ill omen, go to thy hole and hide thy sorry face.' The stranger swallows their insults, and casts toward the bridegroom a beseeching glance.

"But others cry: 'Come on, old man, come on! Come on, fear not the company, the laughing and joking of these pretty gentlemen. Hunt about the tables for the dainties and the carcasses. Hast thou a good jaw? Here, catch this piece of pork and toss off a glass of wine!'

"'No,' at length comes an answer from the old man, in a tone of deep sadness, 'gentlemen, I do not beg, and have never desired what others leave: I seek my son.' —'His son! What is he saying—the son of this seller of eelskins hovering about the Baroness of Aiglun?'

"And they look at each other in doubt, in burning scorn. I listened. Then they said: 'Where is thy son? Show thy son, come on! and beware. If, to mock us, thou lie, wretch, at the highest gargoyle of the towers of Aiglun, without mercy, we'll hang thee!'

"'Well, since I am disowned, and relegated to the sweepings,' the old man begins, draped in his *sayon*, and with a majesty that frightens us, 'you shall hear the crow sing!' Then the Count, turning the color of the wall, cold as a bench of stone, said, 'Varlets, here, cast out this dismal phantom!' Two tears of fire, that pierced the ground, and that I still see shining, streamed down the countenance of the poor old man, ah! so bitter, that we all became white as shrouds.

"'Like Death, I come where I am forgotten, without summons. I am wrong!' broke out the unhappy man, 'but I wished to see my daughter-in-law. Come on, cast out this dismal phantom, who is, however, thy father, O splendid bridegroom!'

"I uttered a cry; all the guests rose from their chairs. But the relentless old man went on: 'My lords, to tear from the evil fruit its whole covering, I have but two words to say. Be seated, for I still see on the table dishes not yet eaten.'

"Standing like palings, silent, anxious, the guests remained with hearts scarce beating. I trembled, my eyes in mist. We were like the dead of the churchyard about some funeral feast, full of terror and mystery. The Count grinned sardonically.

"'Thou shalt run in vain, wretch,' said the venerable father, 'the vengeance of God will surely reach thee! To-day thou makest me bow my head; but thy bride, if she have some honor, will presently flee from thee as from the pest, for thou shalt some day hang, accursed of God!' I rush to the arms of my father-in-law. 'Stop, stop;' but he, leaning down to my ear, said: 'Without knowing the vine or measuring the furrows, thou hast bought the wine, mad girl! Go, thou didst not weep all thy tears in thy swaddling clothes! Knowest thou whom thou hast? a robber-chief!'"

And the scene continues, weirdly dramatic, like some old romantic tale of feudal days. Such scenes of gloom and terror are not frequent in Mistral. This one is probably the best of its kind he has attempted.

On his way to seek Count Sévéran in his fastness, Calendau "enters, awe-struck, into the stupendous valley, deep, frowning, cold, saturnine, and fierce; the daylight darts into this enclosure an instant upon the viper and the lizard, then, behind the jagged peaks, it vanishes. The Esteron rolls below. Now, Calendau feels a shudder in his soul, and winds his horn. The call resounds in the depths of the gorges. It seems as though he calls to his aid the spirits of the place. And he thinks of the paladin dying at Roncevaux."

For the sake of greater completeness, we summarize briefly the exploits of the hero. As has been stated, they compose the great body of the poem, and are narrated by him to the Count and his company of thieves and women. The narrative begins with the account of the little port of Cassis, his native place; and one of the stanzas is a setting for the surprising proverb:—

> "Tau qu'a vist Paris,
> Se noun a vist Cassis,
> Pòu dire: N'ai rèn vist!"

He who has seen Paris, and has not seen Cassis, may say, "I have seen nothing."

No less than forty stanzas are taken up with the wonders of Cassis, and more than half of those are devoted to naming the fish the Cassidians catch. It is to be feared that other than Provençal readers and students of natural history will fail to share the enthusiasm of the poet here. Calendau's father used to read out of an ancient book; and the hero recounts the history of Provence, going back to the times of the Ligurians, telling us of the coming of the Greeks, who brought the art of sculpture for the future Puget. We hear of the founding of Marseilles, the days of Diana and Apollo, followed by the coming of the Romans. The victory of Caius Marius is celebrated, the conquest of Julius Cæsar deplored. We learn of the introduction of Christianity. We come down to the glorious days of Raymond of Toulouse.

"And enraptured to be free, young, robust, happy in the joy of living, in those days a whole people was seen at the feet of Beauty; and singing blame or praises a hundred Troubadours flourished; and from its cradle, amid vicissitudes, Europe smiled upon our merry singing."

"O flowers, ye came too soon! Nation in bloom, the sword cut down thy blossoming! Bright sun of the south, thou shonest too powerfully, and the thunder-storms gathered. Dethroned, made barefoot, and gagged, the Provençal language, proud, however, as before, went off to live among the shepherds and the sailors."

"Language of love, if there are fools and bastards, ah! by Saint Cyr, thou shalt have the men of the land upon thy side, and as long as the fierce mistral shall roar in the rocks, sensitive to an insult offered thee, we shall defend thee with red cannon-balls, for thou art the fatherland, and thou art freedom!"

This love of the language itself pervades all the work of our poet, but rarely has he expressed it more energetically, not to say violently, than here.

Calendau reaches the point where he first catches a glimpse of the Princess. He tells of the legends concerning the fairy Esterello, and of the *Fada* (Les Enfées). This last is a name given to idiots or to the insane, who are supposed to have come under her spell.

> "E degun auso
> Se trufa d'éli, car an quicon de sacra!"

And none dares mock them, for they have in them something sacred.

The fisherman makes many attempts to find her again, and at last succeeds. She haughtily dismisses his suit.

> "Vai, noun sies proun famous, ni proun fort, ni proun fin."

Go, thou art not famous enough, nor strong enough, nor fine enough.

He realizes her great superiority, and, after a time of deep discouragement, rouses himself and sets about to deserve and win her by deeds of daring, by making a great name for himself.

His first idea is to seek wealth, so he builds a great boat and captures twelve hundred tunny fish. The fishing scenes are depicted with all the glow of fancy and brilliant word-painting for which Mistral is so remarkable. Calendau is now rich, and brings jewels to his lady. She haughtily refuses them, and the fisherman throws them away.

> "—Eh! bèn, ié fau, d'abord, ingrato,
> Que toun cor dur ansin me trato
> E que de mi presènt noun t'enchau mai qu' acò,
> Vagon au Diable!—E li bandisse
> Pataflòu! dins lou precepice."...

"Well," said I to her, "since, ungrateful woman, thy hard heart treats me thus, and thou carest no more about my presents than that, let them go to the devil!" and I hurled them, *pataflòu,* into the precipice....

Here the tone is not one that an English reader finds serious; the sending the jewels to the Devil, in the presence of the beautiful lady, and the interjection, seem trivial. Evidently they are not so, for the Princess is mollified at once.

"He was not very astute, he who made thee believe that the love of a proud soul can be won with a few trinkets! Ah, where are the handsome Troubadours, masters of love?"

She tells the love-stories of Geoffroy Rudel, of Ganbert de Puy-Abot, of Foulquet of Marseilles, of Guillaume de Balaün, of Guillaume de la Tour, and her words fall upon Calendau's heart like a flame. He catches a glimpse of an existence of constant ecstasy.

His second exploit is a tournament on the water, where the combatants stand on boats, and are rowed violently against one another, each striking his lance against the wooden breastplate of his adversary. His victory wins for him the hatred of the Cassidians, for his enemy accuses him of cornering the fish. Esterello consoles him with more stories from the *Chansons de geste* and the songs of the Troubadours.

In the seventh canto is described in magnificent language Calendau's exploit on the Mont Ventoux. This is a remarkable mountain, visible all over the southern portion of the Rhone valley, standing in solitary grandeur, like a great pyramid dominating the plain. Its summit is exceedingly difficult of access. It appears to be the first mountain that literature records as having been ascended for pleasure. This ascent is the subject of one of Petrarch's letters.

During nine days Calendau felled the larches that grew upon the flanks of the mighty mountain, and hurled the forest piecemeal into the torrent below. At the Rocher du Cire he is frightfully stung by myriads of bees, during his attempt to obtain as a trophy for his lady a quantity of honey from this well-nigh inaccessible place. The kind of criticism that is appropriate for realistic literature is here quite out of place. It must be said, however, that the episode is far from convincing. Calendau compares his sufferings to those of a soul in hell, condemned to the cauldron of oil. Yet he makes a safe escape, and we never hear of the physical consequences of his terrible punishment.

The canto, in its vivid language, its movement, its life, is one of the most astonishing that has come from the pen of its author. It offers beautiful examples of his inspiration in depicting the lovely aspects of nature. He finds words of liquid sweetness to describe the music of the morning breezes breathing through the mass of trees:—

> "La Ventoureso matiniero,
> En trespirant dins la sourniero
> Dis aubre, fernissié coume un pur cantadis,
> Ounte di colo e di vallado,

Tóuti li voues en assemblado,
Mandavon sa boufaroulado.
Li mèle tranquilas, li mèle mescladis," etc.

The morning breeze of the Mont Ventoux, breathing into the mass of trees, quivered like a pure symphony of song wherein all the voices of hill and dale sent their breathings.

In the last line the word *tranquilas* is meant to convey the idea "in tranquil grandeur."

This ruthless destruction of the forest brings down upon Calendau the anger of his lady; he has dishonored the noble mountain. "Sacrilegious generation, ye have the harvest of the plains, the chestnut and the olives of the hillsides, but the beetling brows of the mountains belong to God!" and the lady continues an eloquent defence of the trees, "the beloved sons, the inseparable nurslings, the joy, the colossal glory of the universal nurse!" and pictures the vengeance Nature wreaks when she is wronged. Calendau is humbled and departs.

His next exploit is the settling of the feud between two orders of Masons. He displays marvellous bravery in facing the fighting crowds, and they choose him to be umpire. He delivers a noble speech in favor of peace, full of allusions to the architectural glories of Provence, that grew up when "faith and union lent their torch." He tells the story of the building of the bridge of Avignon. "Noah himself with his ark could have passed beneath each of its arches." He touches their emotions with his appeal for peace, and they depart reconciled.

And now Esterello begins to love him. She bids him strive for the noblest things, to love country and humanity, to become a knight, an apostle; and after Calendau has performed the feat of capturing the famous brigand Marco-Mau, after he has been crowned in the feasts at Aix, and resisted victorious the wiles of the women that surround the Count Sévéran, and saved his lady in the fearful combat on the fire-surrounded rock, he wins her.

III. NERTO

In spite of its utter unreality *Nerto* is a charming tale, written in a sprightly vein, with here and there a serious touch, reminding the reader frequently of Ariosto. The Devil, the Saints, and the Angels figure in it prominently; but the Devil is not a very terrible personage in Provence, and the Angels are entirely lacking in Miltonic grandeur. The scene of the story is laid in the time of Benedict XIII, who was elected Pope at Avignon in 1394. The story offers a lively picture of the papal court, reminding the reader forcibly of the description found in Daudet's famous tale of the Pope's mule. It is filled throughout with legends relating to the Devil, and with superstitious beliefs of the Middle Age. It is not always easy to determine when the poet is serious in his statement of religious belief, occasionally he appears to be so, and then a line or so shows us that he has a legend in mind. In the prologue of the poem he says:—

"Crèire, coundus à la vitòri.

> Douta, vaqui l' endourmitòri
> E la pouisoun dins lou barriéu
> E la lachuslo dins lou riéu."

To believe leads to victory. Doubt is the narcotic, and the poison in the barrel, and the euphorbia in the stream.

> "E, quand lou pople a perdu fe,
> L'infèr abrivo si boufet."

> And when the people have lost faith,
> Hell sets its bellows blowing.

Then later we read: "What is this world? A wager between Christ and the Demon. Thousands of years ago he challenged God, and when the great game began, they played with great loose rocks from the hills, at quoits, and if any one is unwilling to believe this, let him go to Mount Léberon and see the stone thrown by Satan."

So we see that the theology was merely a means of leading up to a local legend.

The story is briefly as follows: Nerto, like all Mistral's heroines, is exceedingly young, thirteen years of age. Her father, the Baron Pons, had gambled away everything he owned in this world, when she was a very little child, and while walking along a lonely road one night he met the Devil, who took advantage of his despair to tempt him with the sight of heaps of money. The wretched father sold his daughter's soul to the Evil One. Now on his death-bed he tells his child the fearful tale; one means of salvation lies open for her — she must go to the Pope. Benedict XIII is besieged in the great palace at Avignon, but the Baron knows of a secret passage from his castle leading under the river Durance to one of the towers of the papal residence. He bids Nerto go to seek deliverance from the bond, and to make known to the Pope the means of escape. Nerto reaches the palace at the moment when all is in great commotion, for the enemy have succeeded in setting it on fire. She is first seen by the Pope's nephew Don Rodrigue, an exceedingly wicked young man, a sort of brawling Don Juan, who seems to have been guilty of numerous assassinations. He immediately begins to talk love to the maiden, as the means of saving her from the Devil, "the path of love is full of flowers and leads to Paradise." But Nerto has been taught that the road to Heaven is full of stones and thorns, and her innocence saves her from the passionate outburst of the licentious youth. And Nerto is taken to the Pope, whom she finds sadly enthroned in all his splendor, and brings him the news of a means of escape. The last Pope of Avignon bearing the sacred elements, *pourtant soun Diéu*, follows the maiden through the underground passage, and escapes with all his followers. At Château-Renard he sets up his court with the King of Forcalquier, Naples, and Jerusalem and Donna Iolanthe his Queen. Nerto asks the Pope to save her soul, but he is powerless. Only a miracle can save a soul sold to Satan. She must enter a convent, and pray to the Saints continually. The Court is about to move to Arles, she shall enter the convent there. On the way, Don Rodrigue makes love to her assiduously, but the young girl's heart seems untroubled.

At Arles we witness a great combat of animals, in which the lion of Arles, along with four bulls, is turned loose in the arena. The lion kills all but one of the bulls. The fourth beast, enraged, gores the lion. The royal brute rushes among the spectators and makes for the King's throne. Nerto and the Queen are crouching in terror before him, when Don Rodrigue slays the animal, saving Nerto's life. Nay, he saves more than her life, for had she died then she would have been a prey to the flames of Hell.

Nerto becomes a nun, but Don Rodrigue, with a band of ribald followers, succeeds in carrying her off with all the other nuns. They are all driven by the King's soldiers into the cemetery of the Aliscamps. Nerto wanders away during the battle and is lost among the tombs. At dawn the next day she strays far out to a forest, where she finds a hermit. The old man welcomes her, and believes he can save her soul. The Angel Gabriel visits him frequently, and he will speak to him. But the Angel disapproves, condemns the pride of the anchorite, and soars away to the stars without a word of hope or consolation, and so in great anxiety the pious man bids her go back to the convent, and prays Saint Gabriel, Saint Consortia, Saint Tullia, Saint Gent, Saint Verdème, Saint Julien, Saint Trophime, Saint Formin, and Saint Stephen to accompany her.

Don Rodrigue is living in a palace built for him in one night by the Devil, wherein are seven halls, each devoted to one of the seven mortal sins. Hither Nerto wanders; here Rodrigue finds her, and begins his passionate love-making afresh. But Nerto remains true to her vows, although the germ of love has been in her heart since the day Rodrigue saved her from the lion. On learning that she is in the Devil's castle, she is filled with terror, believing the fatal day has arrived. She confesses her love. The maiden cries: "Woe is me, Nerto loves you, but if Hell should swallow us up, would there be any love for the damned? Rodrigue, no, there is none. If you would but break the tie that binds you, if, with one happy wing-stroke, you could soar up to the summits where lives last forever, where hearts vanish united in the bosom of God, I should be delivered, it seems to me, in the same upward impulse; for, in heaven or in the abyss, I am inseparable from you." Rodrigue replies sadly, that his past is too dreadful, that only the ocean could wipe it out. "Rodrigue, one burst of repentance is worth a long penance. Courage, come, only one look toward Heaven!" The Devil appears. He swells with pride in this, his finest triumph; black souls he has in plenty, but since the beginning of his reign over the lower regions he has never captured an immaculate victim like this soul. Rodrigue inverts his sword, and at the sign of the cross, a terrific hurricane sweeps away the palace, Don Rodrigue, and the Devil, and nothing is left but a nun of stone who is still visible in the midst of a field on the site of the château. In an Epilogue we learn from the Archangel who visits the hermit that the knight and the maiden were both saved.

It is difficult to characterize the curious combination of levity and seriousness that runs through this tale. There is no illusion of reality anywhere; there is no agony of soul in Baron Pon's confession; Nerto's terror when she learns that she is the property of the Devil is far from impressive, because she says too much, with expressions that are too pretty, perhaps because the rippling octosyllabic verse, in Provençal at least, cannot be serious; it is hardly worth while to mention the objection that if the Devil can be worsted at any time merely by inverting a sword, especially when the sword is that of an assassin and a rake, whose repentance is scarcely touched upon and is by no means disinterested, it is clear that the Demon has wasted his time at a very foolish game; a religious mind might feel a deeper sort of reverence for the Archangels than is evinced here. Yet it cannot be said that the poem parodies things sacred and sublime, and it appears to be utterly without philosophical intention. Mistral really has to a surprising degree the naïveté of writers of former centuries, and as regards the tale itself and its general treatment it could almost have been written by a contemporary of the events it relates.

IV. LOU POUÈMO DÓU ROSE

The *Poem of the Rhone*, the third of the poems in twelve cantos that Mistral has written, appeared in 1897. It completes the symmetry of his life work; the former epics extolled the life of the fields, the mountains, and the sea, the last glorifies the beautiful river that brings life to his native soil. More than either of the other long poems, it is an act of affection for the past, for the Rhone of the poem is the Rhone of his early childhood, before the steam-packets churned its waters, or the railroads poured up their smoke along its banks. Although the poet has interwoven in it a tale of merest fancy, it is essentially realistic, differing notably in this respect from Calendau. This realism descends to the merest details, and the poetic quality of the work suffers considerably in many passages. The poet does not shrink from minute enumeration of cargoes, or technical description of boats, or word-for-word reproduction of the idle talk of boatwomen, or the apparently inexhaustible profanity of the boatmen. The life on the river is vividly portrayed, and we put down the book with a sense of really having made the journey from Lyons to Beaucaire with the fleet of seven boats of Master Apian.

On opening the volume the reader is struck first of all with the novel versification. It is blank verse, the line being precisely that of Dante's *Divina Commedia*. Not only is there no rhyme, but assonance is very carefully avoided. The effect of this unbroken succession of feminine verses is slightly monotonous, though the poet shifts his pauses skilfully. The rhythm of the lines is marked, the effect upon the ear being quite like that of English iambic pentameters hypercatalectic. The absence of rhyme is the more noteworthy in that rhyme offers little difficulty in Provençal. Doubtless the poet was pleased to show an additional claim to superiority for his speech over the French as a vehicle for poetic thought; for while on the one hand the rules of rhyme and hiatus give the poet writing in Provençal less trouble than when writing in French, on the other hand this poem proves that splendid blank verse may be written in the new language.

The plan of the poem is briefly as follows: it describes the departure of a fleet of boats from Lyons, accompanies them down the river to Beaucaire, describes the fair and the return up the river, the boats being hauled by eighty horses; narrates the collision with a steamboat coming down the stream, which drags the animals into the water, setting the boats adrift in the current, destroying them and their cargo, and typifying as it were the ruin of the old traffic on the Rhone. The river itself is described, its dangerous shoals, its beautiful banks, its towns and castles.

We learn how the boats were manœuvred; the life on board and the ideas of the men are set before us minutely. Legends and stories concerning the river and the places along the shores abound, of course; and into this general background is woven the tale of a Prince of Orange and a little maiden called the Anglore, two of the curiously half-real, half-unreal beings that Mistral seems to love to create. The Prince comes on board the fleet, intending to see Orange and Provence; some day he is to be King of Holland, but has already sickened of court ceremonies and intrigues.

"Uno foulié d'amour s'es mes en tèsto."

This dreamy, imaginative, blond Prince is in search of a Naïade and the mysterious "swan-flower," wherein the fair nymph is hidden. This flower he wears as an emblem. When the boatmen see it, they recognize it as the *fleur de Rhône* that the Anglore is so fond of culling. The men get Jean Roche, one of their number, to tell the Prince who this mysterious Anglore is, and we learn that she is a little, laughing maiden, who wanders barefoot on the sand, so charming that any of the sailors, were she to make a sign, would spring into the water to go and print a kiss upon her little foot. Not only is the Prince in search of a nymph and a flower, not only does he wish to behold Orange, he wishes also to learn the language in which the Countess of Die sang lays of love with Raimbaud of Orange. He is full of thoughts of the olden days, he feels regret for the lost conquests. "But why should he feel regret, if he may recover the sunny land of his forefathers by drinking it in with eager eyes! What need is there of gleaming swords to seize what the eye shows us?" He cares little for royalty.

"Strongholds crumble away, as may be seen on all these hills; everything falls to ruin and is renewed. But on thy summits, unchanging Nature, forever the thyme shall bloom, and the shepherds and shepherdesses frolic on the grass at the return of spring."

The Prince apostrophizes the "empire of the sun," bordering like a silver hem the dazzling Rhone, the "poetic empire of Provence, that with its name alone doth charm the world," and he calls to mind the empire of the Bosonides, the memory of which survives in the speech of the boatmen; they call the east shore "empire," the west shore "kingdom."

The journey is full of episodes. The owner of the fleet, Apian, is a sententious individual. He is devoted to his river life, full of religious fervor, continually crossing himself or praying to Saint Nicholas, the patron saint of sailors. This faith, however, is not entire. If a man falls into the water, the fellows call to him, "Recommend thyself to Saint Nicholas, but swim for dear life." As the English expression has it, "Trust to God, but keep your powder dry." Master Apian always says the Lord's Prayer aloud when he puts off from shore, and solemnly utters the words, "In the name of God and the Holy Virgin, to the Rhone!" His piety, however, does not prevent him from interrupting his prayer to swear at the men most vigorously. Says he, "Let whoever would learn to pray, follow the water," but his arguments and experiences rather teach the vanity of prayer. He is full of superstitious tales. He has views of life.

"Life is a journey like that of the bark. It has its bad, its good days. The wise man, when the waves smile, ought to know how to behave; in the breakers he must go slow. But man is born for toil, for navigation. He who rows gets his pay at the end of the month. He who is afraid of blistering his hands takes a dive into the abyss of poverty." He tells a story of Napoleon in flight down the Rhone, of the women who cried out at him, reviling him, bidding him give back their sons, shaking their fists and crying out, "Into the Rhone with him." Once when he was changing horses at an inn, a woman, bleeding a fowl at the door, exclaimed: "Ha, the cursed monster! If I had him here, I'd plant my knife into his throat like that!" The emperor, unknown to her, draws near. "What did he do to you?" said he. "I had two sons," replied the bereaved mother wrathfully, "two handsome boys, tall as towers. He killed them for me in his battles." —"Their names will not perish in the stars," said Napoleon sadly. "Why could I not fall like them? for they died for their country on the field of glory." —"But who are you?" —"I am the emperor." —"Ah!" The good woman fell upon her knees dismayed, kissed his hands, begged his forgiveness, and all in tears—Here the story is interrupted.

Wholly charming and altogether original is the tale of the little maiden whom the boatmen name L'Anglore, and whom Jean Roche loves. The men have named her so for fun. They knew her well, having seen her from earliest childhood, half naked, paddling in the water along the shore, sunning herself like the little lizard they call *anglore*. Now she had grown, and eked out a poor living by seeking for gold in the sands brought down by the Ardèche.

The little maid believed in the story of the Drac, a sort of merman, that lived in the Rhone, and had power to fascinate the women who ventured into the water. There was once a very widespread superstition concerning this Protean creature; and the women washing in the river often had a figure of the Drac, in the form of a lizard, carved upon the piece of wood with which they beat the linen, as a sort of talisman against his seduction. The mother of the Anglore had told her of his wiles; and one story impressed her above all—the story of the young woman who, fascinated by the Drac, lost her footing in the water and was carried whirling down into the depths. At the end of seven years she returned and told her tale. She had been seized by the Drac, and for seven years he kept her to nurse his little Drac.

The Anglore was never afraid while seeking the specks of gold in the sunlight. But at night it was different. A gem of poetry is the scene in the sixth canto, full of witchery and charm, wherein the imagination of the little maid, wandering out along the water in the mysterious moonlight, causes her to fancy she sees the Drac in the form of a fair youth smiling upon her, offering her a wild flower, uttering sweet, mysterious words of love that die away in the water. She often came again to meet him; and she noticed that if ever she crossed herself on entering the water, as she had always done when a little girl, the Drac would not appear. These three or four pages mark the genuine poet and the master of language. The mysterious night, oppressively warm, the moonlight shining on the little white figure, the deep silence, broken only by the faint murmur of the river and the distant singing of a nightingale, the gleam of the glowworms, compose a scene of fantastic beauty. The slightest sounds startle her, whether it be a fish leaping at the surface of the water to seize a fly, the gurgling of a little eddy, or the shrill cry of a bat. There is a certain voluptuous beauty in the very sound of the words that describe the little nymph, kissed by the moonbeams:—

> "alusentido
> Pèr li rai de la luno que beisavon
> Soun fin coutet, sa jouino car ambrenco,
> Si bras poupin, sis esquino rabloto
> E si pousseto armouniouso e fermo
> Que s'amagavon coume dos tourtouro
> Dins l'esparpai de sa cabeladuro."

The last three lines fall like a caress upon the ear. Mistral often attains a perfect melody of words with the harmonious succession of varied vowel sounds and the well-marked cadence of his verse.

When Apian's fleet comes down the river and passes the spot where the little maid seeks for gold, the men see her and invite her on board. She will go down to Beaucaire to sell her findings. Jean Roche offers himself in marriage, but she will have none of him; she loves the vision seen beneath the waves. When the Anglore spies the blond-haired Prince, she turns pale and nearly swoons. "'Tis he, 'tis he!" she cries, and she stands fascinated. William, charmed with the little maid, says to her, "I recognize thee, O Rhone flower, blooming on the water—flower of good omen that I saw in a dream." The little maid calls him Drac, identifies the flower in his hand, and lives on in this hallucination. The boatmen consider that she has lost her reason, and say she must have drunk of the fountain of Tourne. The little maid hears them, and bids them speak low, for their fate is written at the fountain of Tourne; and like a Sibyl, raising her bare arm, she describes the mysterious carvings on the rock, and the explanation given by a witch she knew. These carvings, according to Mistral's note, were dedicated to the god Mithra. The meaning given by the witch is that the day the Drac shall leave the river Rhone forever, that day the boatmen shall perish. The men do not laugh, for they have already heard of the great boats that can make their way against the current without horses. Apian breaks out into furious imprecations against the men who would ruin the thousands that depend for their living upon the river. One is struck by this introduction of a question of political economy into a poem.

During the journey to Avignon the Prince falls more and more in love with the little Anglore, whom no sort of evidence can shake out of her belief that the Prince is the Drac, for the Drac can assume any form at pleasure. Her delusion is so complete, so naïve, that the prince, romantic by nature, is entirely under the spell.

There come on board three Venetian women, who possess the secret of a treasure, twelve golden statues of the Apostles buried at Avignon. The Prince leaves the boat to help them find the place, and the little maid suffers intensely the pangs of jealousy. But he comes back to her, and takes her all about the great fair at Beaucaire. That night, however, he wanders out alone, and while calling to mind the story of Aucassin and Nicolette, he is sandbagged, but not killed. The Anglore believes he has left his human body on the ground so as to visit his caverns beneath the Rhone. William seems unhurt, and at the last dinner before they start to go up the river again, surrounded by the crew, he makes them a truly Felibrean speech:—

"Do you know, friends, to whom I feel like consecrating our last meal in Beaucaire? To the patriots of the Rhodanian shores, to the dauntless men who, in olden days, maintained themselves in the strong castle that stands before our eyes, to the dwellers along the riverbanks who defended so valiantly their customs, their free trade, and their great free Rhone. If the sons of those forefathers who fell bravely in the strife, to-day have forgotten their glory, well, so much the worse for the sons! But you, my mates, you who have preserved the call, Empire! and who, like the brave men you are, will soon go and defend the Rhone in its very life, fighting your last battle with me, a stranger, but enraptured and intoxicated with the light of your Rhone, come, raise your glasses to the cause of the vanquished!"

The love scenes between the Prince and the Anglore continue during the journey up the river. Her devotion to him is complete; she knows not whither she goes, if to perish, then let it be with him. In a moment of enthusiasm William makes a passionate declaration.

"Trust me, Anglore, since I have freely chosen thee, since thou hast brought me thy deep faith in the beautiful wonders of the fable, since thou art she who, without thought, yields to her love, as wax melts in the sun, since thou livest free of all our bonds and shams, since in thy blood, in thy pure bosom, lies the renewal of the old sap, I, on my faith as a Prince, I swear to thee that none but me, O my Rhone flower, shall have the happiness to pluck thee as a flower of love and as a wife!"

But this promise is never kept. One day the boats meet the steamer coming down the river. Apian, pale and silent, watches the magic bark whose wheels beat like great paws, and, raising great waves, come down steadily upon him.

The captain cries, "One side!" but, obstinate and angry, Apian tries to force the steamer to give way. The result is disastrous. The steamer catches in the towing cables and drags the horses into the water. The boats drift back and are hurled against a bridge. William and the Anglore are thrown into the river and are lost. All the others escape with their lives. Jean Roche is not sure but that he was the Drac after all, who, foreseeing the shipwreck, had thus followed the boats, to carry the Anglore at last down into the depths of the river. Maître Apian accepts his ruin philosophically. Addressing his men, he says: "Ah, my seven boats! my splendid draught horses! All gone, all ruined! It is the end of the business! Poor fellow-boatmen, you may well say, 'good-by to a pleasant life.' To-day the great Rhone has died, as far as we are concerned."

The idea of the poem is, then, to tell of the old life on the Rhone. To-day the river flows almost as in the days when its shores were untrod by men. Rarely is any sort of boat seen upon its swift and dangerous current. Mistral portrays the life he knew, and he has done it with great power and vividness. The fanciful tale of the Prince and the Anglore, suggested by the beliefs and superstitions of the humble folk, was introduced, doubtless, as a necessary love story. The little maid

Anglore, half mad in her illusion, is none the less a very sympathetic creation, and surely quite original. This tale, however, running through the poem like a thread, is not the poem, nor does it fill proportionately a large place therein. The poem is, as its title proclaims, the Poem of the Rhone, a poem of sincere regret for the good old days when the muscular sons of Condrieu ruled the stream, the days of jollity, of the curious boating tournaments of which one is described in *Calendau*, when the children used to watch the boats go by with a Condrillot at the helm, and the Rhone was swarming like a mighty beehive. The poet notes in sorrow that all is dead. The river flows on, broad and silent, and no vestige of all its past activity remains, but here and there a trace of the cables that used to rub along the stones.

As we said at the outset, what is most striking about this poem is its realism. The poet revels in enumerating the good things the men had to eat at the feast of Saint Nicholas; he describes with a wealth of vocabulary and a flood of technical terms quite bewildering every sort of boat, and all its parts with their uses; he reproduces the talk of the boatmen, leaving unvarnished their ignorance and superstition, their roughness and brutality; he describes their appearance, their long hair and large earrings; he explains the manner of guiding the boats down the swirling, treacherous waters, amid the dangers of shoals and hidden rocks; he describes all the cargoes, not finding it beneath the dignity of an epic poem to tell us of the kegs of foamy beer that is destined for the thirsty throats of the drinkers at Beaucaire; as the boats pass Condrieu, he reproduces the gossip of the boatmen's wives; he does not omit the explanations of Apian addressed to the Prince concerning fogs and currents; he is often humorous, telling us of the heavy merchants who promenade their paunches whereon the watch-charms rattle against their snug little money carried in a belt; he describes the passengers, tells us their various trades and destinations, is even cynical; tells of the bourgeois, who, once away from their wives, grow suddenly lavish with their money, and like pigs let loose in the street, take up the whole roadway; he does not shrink from letting us know that the men chew a cud of tobacco while they talk; he mentions the price of goods; he puts into the mouth of Jean Roche's mother a great many practical and material considerations as to the matter of taking a wife, and a very wise and practical old lady she is; he treats as "joyeusetés" the conversation of the Venetian women who inform the Prince that in their city the noblewoman, once married, may have quite a number of lovers without exciting any comment, the husband being rather relieved than otherwise; he allows his boatmen to swear and call one another vile names, and a howling, brawling lot they frequently become; and when at last we get to the fair at Beaucaire, there are pages of minute enumerations that can scarcely be called Homeric. In short, a very large part of the book is prose, animated, vigorous, often exaggerated, but prose. Like his other long poems it is singularly objective. Rarely does the author interrupt his narrative or description to give an opinion, to speak in his own name, or to analyze the situation he has created. Like the other poems, too, it is sprinkled with tales and legends of all sorts, some of them charming. Superstitions abound. Mistral shares the fondness of the Avignonnais for the number seven. Apian has seven boats, the Drac keeps his victim seven years, the woman of Condrieu has seven sons.

The poem offers the same beauties as the others, an astonishing power of description first of all. Mistral is always masterly, always poetic in depicting the landscape and the life that moves thereon, and especially in evoking the life of the past. He revives for us the princesses and queens, the knights and troubadours, and they move before us, a fascinating, glittering pageant. The perfume of flowers, the sunlight on the water, the great birds flying in the air, the silent drifting of the boats in the broad valley, the reflection of the tall poplars in the water, the old ruins that crown the hilltops—all these things are exquisitely woven into the verse, and more than a mere word-painting they create a mood in the reader in unison with the mood of the person of whom he is reading.

In touching truly deep and serious things Mistral is often superficial, and passes them off with a commonplace. An instance in this poem is the episode of the convicts on their way to the galleys at Toulon. No terrible indignation, no heartfelt pity, is expressed. Apian silences one of his crew who attempts to mock at the unhappy wretches. "They are miserable enough without an insult! and do not seem to recognize them, for, branded on the shoulder, they seek the shade. Let this be an example to you all. They are going to eat beans at Toulon, poor fellows! All sorts of men are there,—churchmen, rascals, nobles, notaries, even some who are innocent!"

And the poet concludes, "Thus the world, thus the agitation, the stir of life, good, evil, pleasure, pain, pass along swiftly, confusedly, between day and night, on the river of time, rolling along and fleeing."

The enthusiasm of the poet leads him into exaggeration whenever he comes to a wonder of Provence. Things are relative in this world, and the same words carry different meanings. Avignon is scarcely a colossal pile of towers, and would not remind many of Venice, even at sunset, and we must make a discount when we hear that the boats are *engulfed* in the *fierce* (sic) arch of the *colossal* bridge of stone that Benezet, the shepherd, erected seven hundred years ago. A moment later he refers daintily and accurately to the chapel of Saint Nicholas "riding on the bridge, slender and pretty." The epithets sound larger, too, in Provençal; the view of Avignon is "espetaclouso," the walls of the castle are "gigantesco."

Especially admirable in its sober, energetic expression is the account of the *Remonte*, in the eleventh canto, wherein we see the eighty horses, grouped in fours, tug slowly up the river.

"The long file on the rough-paved path, dragging the weighty train of boats, in spite of the impetuous waters, trudges steadily along. And beneath the lofty branches of the great white poplars, in the stillness of the Rhone valley, in the splendor of the rising sun, walking beside the straining horses that drive a mist from their nostrils, the first driver says the prayer."

With each succeeding poem the vocabulary of Mistral seems to grow, along with the boldness of expression. All his poems he has himself translated into French, and these translations are remarkable in more than one respect. That of the *Poem of the Rhone* is especially full of rare French words, and it cannot be imputed to the leader of the Provençal poets that he is not past master of the French vocabulary. Often his French expression is as strange as the original. Not many French writers would express themselves as he does in the following:—

"Et il tressaille de jumeler le nonchaloir de sa jeunesse au renouveau de la belle ingénue."

In this translation, also, more than in the preceding, there is occasionally an affectation of archaism, which rather adds to than detracts from the poetic effect of his prose, and the number of lines in the prose translation that are really ten-syllable verses is quite remarkable. On one page (page 183 of the third edition, Lemerre) more than half the lines are verses.

Is the *Poem of the Rhone* a great poem? Whether it is or not, it accomplishes admirably the purpose of its author, to fix in beautiful verse the former life of the Rhone. That much of it is prosaic was inevitable; the nature of the subject rendered it so. It is full of beauties, and the poet who wrote *Mirèio* and completed it before his thirtieth year, has shown that in the last decade of his threescore years and ten he could produce a work as full of fire, energy, life, and enthusiasm as in the stirring days when the Félibrige was young. In this poem there occurs a passage put into the mouth of the Prince, which gives a view of life that we suspect is the poet's own. He here calls the Prince a young sage, and as we look back over Mistral's life, and review its aims, and the conditions in which he has striven, we incline to think that here, in a few words, he has condensed his thought.

"For what is life but a dream, a distant appearance, an illusion gliding on the water, which, fleeing ever before our eyes, dazzles us like a mirror flashing, entices and lures us on! Ah, how good it is to sail on ceaselessly toward one's desire, even though it is but a dream! The time will come, it is near, perhaps, when men will have everything within their reach, when they will possess everything, when they will know and have proved everything; and, regretting the old mirages, who knows but what they will not grow weary of living!"

CHAPTER II

LIS ISCLO D'OR

The lover of poetry will probably find more to admire and cherish in this volume than in any other that has come from the pen of its author, excepting, possibly, the best passages of *Mirèio*. It is the collection of his short poems that appeared from time to time in different Provençal publications, the earliest dating as far back as 1848, the latest written in 1888. They are a very complete expression of his poetic ideas, and contain among their number gems of purest poesy. The poet's lyre has not many strings, and the strains of sadness, of pensive melancholy, are almost absent. Mistral has once, and very successfully, tried the theme of Lamartine's *Lac*, of Musset's *Souvenir*, of Hugo's *Tristesse d'Olympio*; but his poem is not an elegy, it has not the intensity, the passion, the deep undertone of any of the three great Romanticists. *La Fin dóu Meissounié* is a beautiful, pathetic, and touching tale, that easily brings a tear, and *Lou Saume de la Penitènci* is without doubt one of the noblest poems inspired in the heart of any Frenchman by the disaster of 1870. But these poems, though among the best according to the feeling for poetry of a reader from northern lands, are not characteristic of the volume in general. The dominant strain is energy, a clarion-call of life and light, an appeal to his fellow-countrymen to be strong and independent; the sun of Provence, the language of Provence, the ideals of Provence, the memories of Provence, these are his themes. His poetry is not personal, but social. Of his own joys and sorrows scarce a word, unless we say what is doubtless the truth, that his joys and sorrows, his regrets and hopes, are identical with those of his native land, and that he has blended his being completely with the life about him. The volume contains a great number of pieces written for special occasions, for the gatherings of the Félibres, for their weddings. Many of them are addressed to persons in France and out, who have been in various ways connected with the Félibrige. Of these the greeting to Lamartine is especially felicitous in expression, and the following stanza from it forms the dedication of *Mirèio*:—

> "Te counsacre Mirèio: eo moun cor e moun amo,
> Es la flour de mis an;
> Es un rasin de Crau qu' emé touto sa ramo
> Te porge un païsan."

The entire poem, literally translated, is as follows:—

> If I have the good fortune to see my bark early upon the waves,
> Without fear of winter,

Blessings upon thee, O divine Lamartine,
Who hast taken the helm!

If my prow bears a bouquet of blooming laurel,
It is thou hast made it for me;
If my sail swelleth, it is the breath of thy glory
That bloweth it.

Therefore, like a pilot who of a fair church
Climbeth the hill
And upon the altar of the saint that hath saved him at sea
Hangeth a miniature ship.

I consecrate Mirèio to thee; 'tis my heart and my soul,
'Tis the flower of my years;
'Tis a cluster of grapes from the Crau that with all its leaves
A peasant offers thee.

Generous as a king, when thou broughtest me fame
In the midst of Paris,
Thou knowest that, in thy home, the day thou saidst to me,
"Tu Marcellus eris!"

Like the pomegranate in the ripening sunbeam,
My heart opened,
And, unable to find more tender speech,
Broke out in tears.

It is interesting to notice that the earliest poem of our author, *La Bella d'Avoust*, is a tale of the supernatural, a poem of mystery; it is an order of poetic inspiration rather rare in his work, and this first poem is quite as good as anything of its kind to be found in *Mirèio* or *Nerto*. It has the form of a song with the refrain:—

Ye little nightingales, ye grasshoppers, be still!
Hear the song of the beauty of August!

Margaï of Val-Mairane, intoxicated with love, goes down into the plain two hours before the day. Descending the hill, she is wild. "In vain," she says, "I seek him, I have missed him. Ah, my heart trembles."

The poem is full of imagery, delicate and pretty. Margaï is so lovely that in the clouds the moon, enshrouded, says to the cloud very softly, "Cloud, beautiful cloud, pass away, my face would let fall a ray on Margaï, thy shadow hinders me." And the bird offers to console her, and the glow-worm offers his light to guide her to her lover. Margaï comes and goes until she meets her lover in the shadow of the trees. She tells of her weeping, of the moon, the birdling, and the glow-worm. "But thy brow is dark, art thou ill? Shall I return to my father's house?"

"If my face is sad, on my faith, it is because a black moth hovering about hath alarmed me."

And Margaï says, "Thy voice, once so sweet, to-day seems a trembling sound beneath the earth; I shudder at it."

"If my voice is so hoarse, it is because while waiting for thee I lay upon my back in the grass."

"I was dying with longing, but now it is with fear. For the day of our elopement, beloved, thou wearest mourning!"

"If my cloak be sombre and black, so is the night, and yet the night also glimmers."

When the star of the shepherds began to pale, and when the king of stars was about to appear, suddenly off they went, upon a black horse. And the horse flew on the stony road, and the ground shook beneath the lovers, and 'tis said fantastic witches danced about them until day, laughing loudly.

Then the white moon wrapped herself again, the birdling on the branch flew off in fright, even the glow-worm, poor little thing, put out his lamp, and quickly crept away under the grass. And it is said that at the wedding of poor Margaï there was little feasting, little laughing, and the betrothal and the dancing took place in a spot where fire was seen through the crevices.

"Vale of Val-Mairane, road to the Baux, never again o'er hill or plain did ye see Margaï. Her mother prays and weeps, and will not have enough of speaking of her lovely shepherdess."

This weird, legendary tale was composed in 1848. The next effort of the poet is one of his masterpieces, wherein his inspiration is truest and most poetical. *La Fin dóu Meissounié* (The Reaper's Death) is a noble, genuinely pathetic tale, told in beautifully varied verse, full of the love of field work, and aglow with sympathy for the toilers. The figure of the old man, stricken down suddenly by an accidental blow from the scythe of a young man mowing behind him, as he lies dying on the rough ground, urging the gleaners to go on and not mind him, praying to Saint John, — the patron of the harvesters, — is one not to be forgotten. The description of the mowing, the long line of toilers with their scythes, the fierce sun making their blood boil, the sheaves falling by hundreds, the ruddy grain waving in the breath of the mistral, the old chief leading the band, "the strong affection that urged the men on to cut down the harvest," — all is vividly pictured, and foretells the future poet of *Mirèio*. The words of the old man are full of his energy and faith: "The wheat, swollen and ripe, is scattering in the summer wind; do not leave to the birds and ants, O binders, the wheat that comes from God!" "What good is your weeping? better sing with the young fellows, for I, before you all, have finished my task. Perhaps, in the land where I shall be presently, it will be hard for me, when evening comes, to hear no more, stretched out upon the grass, as I used to, the strong, clear singing of the youth rising up amid the trees; but it appears, friends, that it was my star, or perhaps the Master, the One above, seeing the ripe grain, gathers it in. Come, come, good-by, I am going gently. Then, children, when you carry off the sheaves upon the cart, take away your chief on the load of wheat."

And he begs Saint John to remember his olive trees, his family, who will sup at Christmas-tide without him. "If sometimes I have murmured, forgive me! The sickle, meeting a stone, cries out, O master Saint John, the friend of God, patron of the reapers, father of the poor, up there in Paradise, remember me."

And after the old man's death "the reapers, silent, sickle in hand, go on with the work in haste, for the hot mistral was shaking the ears."

Among these earlier poems are found some cleverly told, homely tales, with a pointed moral. Such are *La Plueio* (The Rain), *La Rascladuro de Petrin* (The Scraping from the Kneading-trough). They are really excellent, and teach the lesson that the tillers of the soil have a holy calling, of which they may be proud, and that God sends them health and happiness, peace and liberty. The second of the poems just mentioned is a particularly amusing story of choosing a wife according to the care she takes of her kneading-trough, the idea being derived from an old fablieau. There are one or two others purely humorous and capitally told. After 1860, however, the poet abandoned these homely, simple tales, that doubtless realized Roumanille's ideas of one aspect of the literary revival he was seeking to bring about.

The poems are not arranged chronologically, but are classified as Songs, Romances, Sirventés, Reveries, Plaints, Sonnets, Nuptial Songs, etc.

The *Cansoun* (Songs) are sung at every reunion of the Félibrige. They are set to melodies well known in Provence, and are spirited and vigorous indeed. The Germans who write about Provence are fond of making known the fact that the air of the famous *Hymn to the Sun* is a melody written by Kuecken. There is *Lou Bastimen* (The Ship), as full of dash and go as any English sea ballad. *La Coutigo* (The Tickling) is a dialogue between a mother and her love-sick son. *La Coupo* (The Cup) is the song of the Félibres *par excellence*; it was composed for the reception of a silver cup, sent to the Félibres by the Catalans. The *coupo felibrenco* is now a feature of all their banquets. The song expresses the enthusiasm of the Félibres for their cause. The refrain is, "Holy cup, overflowing, pour out in plenty the enthusiasms and the energy of the strong." The most significant lines are:—

> Of a proud, free people
> We are perhaps the end;
> And, if the Félibres fall,
> Our nation will fall.

> Of a race that germs anew
> Perhaps we are the first growth;
> Of our land we are perhaps
> The pillars and the chiefs.

> Pour out for us hope
> And dreams of youth,
> The memory of the past
> And faith in the coming year.

The ideas and sentiments, then, that are expressed in the shorter poems of Mistral, written since the publication of *Mirèio*, have been, in the main, the ancient glories and liberties of Provence, a clinging to national traditions, to local traditions, and to the religion and ideas of ancestors, a profound dislike of certain modern ideas of progress, hatred of the levelling influence of Paris, love of the Provençal speech, belief in the Latin race, in the Roman Catholic Church, unshaken faith in the future, love of the ideal and hatred of what is servile and sordid, an ardent love of Nature, an intense love of life and movement. These things are reflected in every variety of word and figure. He is not the poet of the romantic type, self-centred, filling his verse with the echoes of his own loves and joys and woes, nor is his poetry as large as humanity; Provence, France, the Latin race, are the limits beyond which it has no message or interest.

Possibly no poet ever wrote as many lines to laud the language he was using. Such lines abound in each volume he has produced.

> "Se la lengo di moussu
> Toumbo en gargavaio
> Se tant d'escrivan coussu
> Pescon de ravaio,
> Nàutri, li bon Prouvençau
> Vers li serre li plus aut
> Enauren la lengo
> De nòsti valengo."

If the language of the messieurs falls among the sweepings, if so many comfortably well-off writers fish for small fry, we, the good Provençals, toward the highest summits, raise the language of our valleys.

The Sirventés addressed to the Catalan poets begins:—

> "Fraire de Catalougno, escoutas! Nous an di
> Que fasias peralin reviéure e resplendi
> Un di rampau de nosto lengo."

Brothers from Catalonia, listen! We have heard that ye cause one of the branches of our language to revive and flourish yonder.

In the same poem, the poet sings of the Troubadours, whom none have since surpassed, who in the face of the clergy raised the language of the common people, sang in the very ears of the kings, sang with love, and sang freely, the coming of a new world and contempt for ancient fears, and later on he says:—

"From the Alps to the Pyrenees, hand in hand, poets, let us then raise up the old Romance speech! It is the sign of the family, the sacrament that binds the sons to the forefathers, man to the soil! It is the thread that holds the nest in the branches. Fearless guardians of our beautiful speech, let us keep it free and pure, and bright as silver, for a whole people drinks at this spring; for when, with faces on the ground, a people falls into slavery, if it holds its language, it holds the key that delivers it from the chains."

The final stanza of the poem, written in honor of Jasmin in 1870, is as follows:—

"For our dead and our fathers, and our sacred rights as a people and as poets, that yesterday were trampled beneath the feet of the usurper, and, outraged, cried out, now live again in glory! Now, between the two seas the language of Oc triumphs. O Jasmin, thou hast avenged us!"

In the *Rock of Sisyphus* the poet says, "Formerly we kept the language that Nature herself put upon our lips."

In the *Poem to the Latin Race* we read:—

"Thy mother tongue, the great stream that spreads abroad in seven branches, pouring out love and light like an echo from Paradise, thy golden speech, O Romance daughter of the King-People, is the song that will live on human lips as long as speech shall have reason."

Elsewhere we find:—

"Oh, maintain thy historic speech. It is the proof that always thou carriest on high and free, thy coat of arms. In the language, a mystery, an old treasure is found. Each year the nightingale puts on new plumage, but keeps its song."

One entire poem, *Espouscado*, is a bitterly indignant protest against those who would suppress the dialect, against the regents and the rectors whom "we must pay with our pennies to hear them scoff at the language that binds us to our fathers and our soil!" And the poet cries out, "No, no, we'll keep our rebellious *langue d'oc*, grumble who will. We'll speak it in the stables, at harvest-time, among the silkworms, among lovers, among neighbors, etc., etc. It shall be the language of joy and of brotherhood. We'll joke and laugh with it;—and as for the army, we'll take it to the barracks to keep off homesickness."

And his anger rising, he exclaims:—

"O the fools, the fools, who wean their children from it to stuff them with self-sufficiency, fatuity, and hunger! Let them get drowned in the throng! But thou, O my Provence, be not disturbed about the sons that disown thee and repudiate thy speech. They are dead, they are still-born children that survive, fed on bad milk."

And he concludes:—

"But, eldest born of Nature, you, the sun-browned boys, who speak with the maidens in the ancient tongue, fear not; you shall remain the masters! Like the walnuts of the plain, gnarled, stout, calm, motionless, exploited and ill-treated as you may be, O peasants (as they call you), you will remain masters of the land!"

This was written in 1888. The quotations might be multiplied; these suffice, however, to show the intense love of the poet for "the language of the soil," the energy with which he has constantly struggled for its maintenance. He is far from looking upon the multiplication of dialects as an evil, points to the literary glory of Greece amid her many forms of speech, and does not even seek to impose his own language upon the rest of southern France. He sympathizes with every attempt, wherever made, the world over, to raise up a patois into a language. Statesmen will probably think otherwise, and there are nations which would at once take an immense stride forward if they could attain one language and a purely national literature. The modern world does not appear to be marching in accordance with Mistral's view.

The poems inspired by the love of the ancient ideals and literature of Provence are very beautiful. They have in general a fascinating swing and rhythm, and are filled with charming imagery. One of the best is *L'Amiradou* (The Belvedere), the story of a fairy imprisoned in the castle at Tarascon, "who will doubtless love the one who shall free her." Three knights attempt the rescue and fail. Then there comes along a little Troubadour, and sings so sweetly of the prowess of his forefathers, of the splendor of the Latin race, that the guard are charmed and the bolts fly back. And the fairy goes up to the top of the tower with the little Troubadour, and they stand mute with love, and look out over all the beautiful landscape, and the old monuments of Provence with their lessons. This is the kingdom of the fairy, and she bestows it upon him. "For he who knows how to read in this radiant book, must grow above all others, and all that his eye beholds, without paying any tithe, is his in abundance."

The lilt of this little *romance*, with its pretty repetitions, is delightful, and the symbolism is, of course, perfectly obvious.

There is the touching story of the Troubadour Catalan, slain by robbers in the Bois de Boulogne, where the Pré de Catalan now is; there is the tale that accounts for the great chain that hangs across the gorge at Moustiers, a chain over six hundred feet long, bearing a star in the centre. A knight, being prisoner among the Saracens, vows to hang the chain before the chapel of the Virgin, if ever he returns home.

> "A ti pèd, vierge Mario,
> Ma cadeno penjarai,
> Se jamai
> Tourne mai
> A Moustié, dins ma patrio!"

There is the tale of the Princess Clémence, daughter of a king of Provence. Her father was deformed, and the heir-presumptive to the French crown sought her in marriage. In order that the prince might be sure she had inherited none of the father's deformity, she was called upon to show herself in the garb of Lady Godiva before his ambassadors. This rather delicate subject is handled with consummate art.

The idea of federalism is found expressed with sufficient clearness in various parts of these poems of the Golden Isles, and the patriotism of the poet, his love of France, is perfectly evident, in spite of all that has been said to the contrary. In the poem addressed to the Catalans, after numerous allusions to the dissensions and rebellions of bygone days, we read:—

"Now, however, it is clear; now, however, we know that in the divine order all is for the best; the Provençals, a unanimous flame, are part of great France, frankly, loyally; the Catalans, with good-will, are part of magnanimous Spain. For the brook must flow to the sea, and the stone must fall on the heap; the wheat is best protected from the treacherous cold wind when planted close; and the little boats, if they are to navigate safely, when the waves are black and the air dark, must sail together. For it is good to be many, it is a fine thing to say, 'We are children of France!'"

But in days of peace let each province develop its own life in its own way.

"And France and Spain, when they see their children warming themselves together in the sunbeams of the fatherland, singing matins out of the same book, will say, 'The children have sense enough, let them laugh and play together, now they are old enough to be free.'

"And we shall see, I promise you, the ancient freedom come down, O happiness, upon the smallest city, and love alone bind the races together; and if ever the black talon of the tyrant is seen, all the races will bound up to drive out the bird of prey!"

Of all the poems of Mistral expressing this order of ideas, the one entitled *The Countess* made the greatest stir. It appeared in 1866, and called forth much angry discussion and imputation of treason from the enemies of the new movement. *The Countess* is an allegorical representation of Provence; the fair descendant of imperial ancestors is imprisoned in a convent by her half-sister France. Formerly she possessed a hundred fortified towns, twenty seaports; she had olives, fruit, and grain in abundance; a great river watered her fields; a great wind vivified the land, and the proud noblewoman could live without her neighbor, and she sang so sweetly that all loved her, poets and suitors thronged about her.

Now, in the convent where she is cloistered all are dressed alike, all obey the rule of the same bell, all joy is gone. The half-sister has broken her tambourines and taken away her vineyards, and gives out that her sister is dead.

Then the poet breaks into an appeal to the strong to break into the great convent, to hang the abbess, and say to the Countess, "Appear again, O splendor! Away with grief, away! Long life to joy!"

Each stanza is followed by the refrain:—

> "Ah! se me sabien entèndre!
> Ah! se me voulien segui!"

> Ah! if they could understand me!
> Ah! if they would follow me!

Mistral disdained to reply to the storm of accusations and incriminations raised by the publication of this poem. *Lou Saumede la Penitènci*, that appeared in 1870, set at rest all doubts concerning his deep and sincere patriotism.

The Psalm of Penitence is possibly the finest of the short poems. It is certainly surpassed by no other in intensity of feeling, in genuine inspiration, in nobility and beauty of expression. It is a hymn of sorrow over the woes of France, a prayer of humility and resignation after the disaster of 1870. The reader must accept the idea, of course, that the defeat of the French was a visitation of Providence in punishment for sin.

> "Segnour, à la fin ta coulèro
> Largo si tron
> Sus nòsti front:
> E dins la niue nosto galèro
> Pico d'a pro
> Contro li ro."

Lord, at last thy wrath hurls its thunderbolts upon our foreheads:
And in the night our vessel strikes its prow against the rocks.

France was punished for irreligion, for closing the temples, for abandoning the sacraments and commandments, for losing faith in all except selfish interest and so-called progress, for contempt of the Bible and pride in science.

The poet makes confession:—

"Segnour, sian tis enfant proudigue;
Mai nàutri sian
Ti vièi crestian:
Que ta Justiço nous castigue,
Mai au trepas
Nous laisses pas!"

Lord, we are thy prodigal sons; but we are thy Christians of old:
Let thy justice chastise us, but give us not over unto death!

Then the poet prays in the name of all the brave men who gave up their lives in battle, in the name of all the mothers who will never again see their sons, in the name of the poor, the strong, the dead, in the name of all the defeats and tears and sorrow, the slaughter and the fires, the affronts endured, that God disarm his justice, and he concludes:—

"Segnour, voulen deveni d'ome;
En libertà
Pos nous bouta!
Sian Gau-Rouman e gentilome,
E marchan dre
Dins noste endré.

"Segnour, dóu mau sian pas Pencauso.
Mando eiçabas
Un rai de pas!
Segnour, ajudo nosto Causo,
E reviéuren
E t'amaren."

Lord, we desire to become men; thou canst set us free!
We are Gallo-Romans and of noble race, and we walk upright in our land.
Lord, we are not the cause of the evil. Send down upon us a ray of peace!
Lord, aid our Cause, and we shall live again and love thee.

The poem called *The Stone of Sisyphus* completes sufficiently the evidence necessary to exculpate Mistral of the charge of antipatriotism and makes clear his thought. Provence was once a nation, she consented years ago to lose her identity in the union with France. Now it is proposed to heap up all the old traditions, the Gai Savoir, the glory of the Troubadours, the old language, the old customs, and burn them on a pyre. Well, France is a great people and *Vive la nation*. But some would go further, some would suppress the nation: "Down with the frontiers, national glories are an abomination! Wipe out the past, man is God! *Vive l'humanité!*" Our patrimony we repudiate. What are Joan of Arc, Saint Louis, and Turenne? All that is old rubbish.

Then the people cry with Victor Hugo, *"Emperaire, siegues maudi, maudi, maudi! nous as vendu"* and hurl down the Vendôme column, burn Paris, slaughter the priests, and then, worn out, commence again, like Sisyphus, to push the rock of progress.

So much for the conservatism of Mistral.

We shall conclude this story of the shorter poems with some that are not polemical or essentially Provençal; three or four are especially noteworthy. *The Drummer of Arcole, Lou Prègo-Diéu, Rescontre* (Meeting), might properly find a place in any anthology of general poetry, and an ode on the death of Lamartine is sincere and beautiful. Such poems must be read in the original.

The first one, *The Drummer of Arcole*, is the story of a drummer boy who saved the day at Arcole by beating the charge; but after the wars are over, he is forgotten, and remains a drummer as before, becomes old and regrets his life given up to the service of his country. But one day, passing along the streets of Paris, he chances to look up at the Pantheon, and there in the huge pediment he reads the words, *"Aux grands hommes la patrie reconnaissante."*

"'Drummer, raise thy head!' calls out a passer-by! 'The one up there, hast thou seen him?' Toward the temple that stood superb the old man raised his bewildered eyes. Just then the joyous sun shook his golden locks above enchanted Paris...."

"When the soldier saw the dome of the Pantheon rising toward heaven, and with his drum hanging at his side, beating the charge, as if it were real, he recognized himself, the boy of Arcole, away up there, right at the side of the great Napoleon, intoxicated with his former fury, seeing himself, so high, in full relief, above the years, the clouds, the storms, in glory, azure, sunshine, he felt a gentle swelling in his heart, and fell dead upon the pavement."

Lou Prègo-Diéu is a sweet poem embodying a popular belief. Prègo-diéu is the name of a little insect, so called from the peculiar arrangement of its legs and antennse that makes it appear to be in an attitude of prayer. Mistral's poetic ideas have been largely suggested to him by popular beliefs and the stories he heard at his fireside when a boy. This poem is one of the best of the kind he has produced, and, being eminently, characteristic, will find juster treatment in a literal translation than in a commentary. The first half was written during the time he was at work upon *Mirèio* in 1856, the second in 1874. We quote the first stanza in the original, for the sake of showing its rhythm.

> "Ero un tantost d'aquel estiéu
> Que ni vihave ni dourmiéu:
> Fasiéu miejour, tau que me plaise,
> Lou cahessòu
> Toucant lou sòn
> A l'aise."

I

It was one afternoon this summer, while I was neither awake nor asleep. I was taking a noon siesta, as is my pleasure, my head at ease upon the ground.

And greenish among the stubble, upon a spear of blond barley, with a double row of seeds, I saw a prègo-diéu.

"Beautiful insect," said I, "I have heard that, as a reward for thy ceaseless praying, God hath given thee the gift of divination.

"Tell me now, good friend, if she I love hath slept well; tell what she is thinking at this hour, and what she is doing; tell me if she is laughing or weeping."

The insect, that was kneeling, stirred upon the tube of the tiny, leaning ear, and unfolded and waved his little wings.

And his speech, softer than the softest breath of a zephyr wafted in a wood, sweet and mysterious, reached my ear.

"I see a maiden," said he, "in the cool shade beneath a cherry tree; the waving branches touch her; the boughs hang thick with cherries.

"The cherries are fully ripe, fragrant, solid, red, and, amid the smooth leaves, make one hungry, and, hanging, tempt one.

"But the cherry tree offers in vain the sweetness and the pleasing color of its bright, firm fruit, red as coral.

"She sighs, trying to see if she can jump high enough to pluck them. Would that my lover might come! He would climb up, and throw them down into my apron."

So I say to the reapers: "Reapers, leave behind you a little corner uncut, where, during the summer, the prègo-diéu may have shelter."

II

This autumn, going down a sunken road, I wandered off across the fields, lost in earthly thoughts.

And, once more, amid the stubble, I saw, clinging to a tiny ear of grain, folded up in his double wing, the prègo-diéu.

"Beautiful insect," said I then, "I have heard that, as a reward for thy ceaseless praying, God hath given thee the gift of divination.

"And that if some child, lost amid the harvest fields, asks of thee his way, thou, little creature, showest him the way through the wheat.

"In the pleasures and pains of this world, I see that I, poor child, am astray; for, as he grows, man feels his wickedness.

"In the grain and in the chaff, in fear and in pride, in budding hope, alas for me, I see my ruin.

"I love space, and I am in chains; among thorns I walk barefoot; Love is God, and Love sins; every enthusiasm after action is disappointed.

"What we accomplished is wiped out; brute instinct is satisfied, and the ideal is not reached; we must be born amid tears, and be stung among the flowers.

"Evil is hideous, and it smiles upon me; the flesh is fair, and it rots; the water is bitter, and I would drink; I am languishing, I want to die and yet to live.

"I am falling faint and weary; O prègo-diéu, cause some slight hope of something true to shine upon me; show me the way."

And straightway I saw that the insect stretched forth its slender arm toward Heaven; mysterious, mute, earnest, it was praying.

Such reference to religious doubt is elsewhere absent from Mistral's work. His faith is strong, and the energy of his life-work has its source largely, not only in this religious faith, but in his firm belief in himself, in his race, and in the mission he has felt called upon to undertake. Reflected obviously in the above poem is the growth of the poet in experience and in thought.

Lastly, among the poems of his *Isclo d'Or*, we wish to call attention to one that, in its theme, recalls *Le Lac*, *La Tristesse d'Olympio*, and *Le Souvenir*. The poet comes upon the scene of his first love, and apostrophizes the natural objects about him. All four poets intone the strain, "Ye rocks and trees, guard the memory of our love."

> "O coumbo d'Uriage
> Bos fresqueirous,
> Ounte aven fa lou viage
> Dis amourous,
> O vau qu'aven noumado
> Noste univers,
> Se perdes ta ramado
> Gardo mi vers."

O vale of Uriage, cool wood, where we made our lovers' journey; O vale that we called our world, if thou lose thy verdure, keep my verses.

Ye flowers of the high meadows that no man knoweth, watered by Alpine snows, ye are less pure and fresh in the month of April than the little mouth that smiles for me.

Ye thunders and stern voices of the peaks, murmurings of wild woods, torrents from the mountains, there is a voice that dominates you all, the clear, beautiful voice of my love.

Alas! vale of Uriage, we may never return to thy leafy nooks. She, a star, vanisheth in air, and I, folding my tent, go forth into the wilderness.

Apart from the intrinsic worth of the thought or sentiment, there is found in Mistral the essential gift of the poet, the power of expression—of clothing in words that fully embody the meaning, and seem to sing, in spontaneous musical flow, the inner inspiration. He is superior to the other poets of the Félibrige, not only in the energy, the vitality of his personality, and in the fertility of his ideas, but also in this great gift of language. Even if he creates his vocabulary as he goes along, somewhat after the fashion of Ronsard and the *Pléiade*, he does this in strict accordance with the genius of his dialect, fortunately for him, untrammelled by traditions, and, what is significant, he does it acceptably. He is the master. His fellow-poets proclaim and acclaim his supremacy. No one who has penetrated to any degree into the genius of the Romance languages can fail to agree that in this point exists a master of one of its forms.

CHAPTER III
THE TEAGEDY, LA RÈINO JANO

The peculiar qualities and limitations of Mistral are possibly nowhere better evidenced than in this play. Full of charming passages, frequently eloquent, here and there very poetic, it is scarcely dramatic, and certainly not a tragedy either of the French or the Shakespearian type. The most striking lines, the most eloquent tirades, arise less from the exigences of the drama than from the constant desire of the poet to give expression to his love of Provence. The attention of the reader is diverted at every turn from the adventures of the persons in the play to the glories and the beauties of the lovely land in which our poet was born. The matter of a play is certainly contained in the subject, but the energy of the author has not been spent upon the invention of strong situations, upon the clash of wills, upon the psychology of his characters, upon the interplay of passions, but rather upon strengthening in the hearts of his Provençal hearers the love of the good Queen Joanna, whose life has some of the romance of that of Mary, Queen of Scots, and upon letting them hear from her lips and from the lips of her courtiers the praises of Provence.

Mistral enumerates eight dramatic works treating the life of his heroine. They are a tragedy in five acts and a verse by Magnon (Paris, 1656), called *Jeanne Ire, reine de Naples*; a tragedy in five acts and in verse by Laharpe, produced in 1781, entitled, *Jeanne de Naples*; an opéra-comique in three acts, the book by De Leuven and Brunswick, the music by Monpon and Bordèse, produced in 1840; an Italian tragedy, *La Regina Griovanna*, by the Marquis of Casanova, written about 1840; an Italian opera, the libretto by Ghislanzoni, who is known as the librettist of *Aïda*, the music by Petrella (Milan, 1875); a play in verse by Brunetti, called *Griovanna I di Napoli* (Naples, 1881); a Hungarian play by Rakosi, *Johanna es Endre*, and lastly the trilogy of Walter Savage Landor, *Andrea of Hungary, Griovanna of Naples*, and *Fra Rupert* (London, 1853). Mistral's play is dated May, 1890.

It may be said concerning the work of Landor, which is a poem in dramatic form rather than a play, that it offers scarcely any points of resemblance with Mistral's beyond the few essential facts in the lives of Andrea and Joanna. Both poets take for granted the innocence of the Queen. It is worth noting that Provence is but once referred to in the entire work of the English poet.

The introduction that precedes Mistral's play quotes the account of the life of the Queen from the *Dictionnaire* of Moréri (Lyons, 1681), which we here translate.

"Giovanna, first of the name, Queen of Jerusalem, Naples, and Sicily, Duchess of Apulia and Calabria, Countess of Provence, etc., was a daughter of Charles of Sicily, Duke of Calabria, who died in 1328, before his father Robert, and of Marie of Valois, his second wife. She was only nineteen years of age when she assumed the government of her dominions after her grandfather's death in 1343. She had already been married by him to his nephew, Andrea of Hungary. This was not a happy marriage; for the inclinations of both were extremely contrary, and the prince was controlled by a Franciscan monk named Robert, and the princess by a washerwoman called Filippa Catenese. These indiscreet advisers brought matters to extremes, so that Andrea was strangled in 1345. The disinterested historians state ingenuously that Joanna was not guilty of this crime, although the others accuse her of it. She married again, on the 2d of August, 1346. Her second husband was Louis of Tarento, her cousin; and she was obliged to leave Naples to avoid the armed attack of Louis, King of Hungary, who committed acts of extreme violence in this state. Joanna, however, quieted all these things by her prudence, and after losing this second husband, on the 25th of March, 1362, she married not long afterward a third, James of Aragon, Prince of Majorca, who, however, tarried not long with her. So seeing herself a widow for the third time, she made a fourth match in 1376 with Otto of Brunswick, of the House of Saxony; and as she had no children, she adopted a relative, Charles of Duras.... This ungrateful prince revolted against Queen Joanna, his benefactress.... He captured Naples, and laid siege to the Castello Nuovo, where the Queen was. She surrendered. Charles of Duras had her taken to Muro, in the Basilicata, and had her put to death seven or eight months afterward. She was then in her fifty-eighth year.... Some authors say that he caused her to be smothered, others that she was strangled; but the more probable view is that she was beheaded, in 1382, on the 5th of May. It is said that a Provençal astrologer, doubtless a certain Anselme who lived at that time, and who is very famous in the history of Provence, being questioned as to the future husband of the young princess, replied, 'Maritabitur cum ALIO.' This word is composed of the initials of the names of her four husbands, Andrea, Louis, James, and Otto. This princess, furthermore, was exceedingly clever, fond of the sciences and of men of learning, of whom she had a great many at her court, liberal and beautiful, prudent, wise, and not lacking in piety. She it is that sold Avignon to the popes. Boccaccio, Balde, and other scholars of her time speak of her with praise."

In offering an explanation of the great popularity enjoyed by Joanna of Naples among the people of Provence, the poet does not hesitate to acknowledge that along with her beauty, her personal charm, her brilliant arrival on the gorgeous galley at the court of Clement VI, whither she came, eloquent and proud, to exculpate herself, her long reign and its vicissitudes, her generous efforts to reform abuses, must be counted also the grewsome procession of her four husbands; and this popularity, he says, is still alive, after five centuries. The poet places her among such historic figures as Caius Marius, Ossian, King Arthur, Count Raymond of Toulouse, the good King René, Anne of Brittany, Roland, the Cid, to which the popular mind has attached heroic legends, race traditions, and mysterious monuments. The people of Provence still look back upon the days of their independence when she reigned, a sort of good fairy, as the good old times of Queen Joanna. Countless castles, bridges, churches, monuments, testify to her life among this enthusiastic people. Roads and ruins, towers and aqueducts, bear her name. Proverbs exist wherein it is preserved. "For us," says Mistral, "the fair Joanna is what Mary Stuart is for the Scotch,—a mirage of retrospective love, a regret of youth, of nationality, of poetry passed away. And analogies are not lacking in the lives of the two royal, tragic enchantresses." Petrarch, speaking of her and her young husband surrounded by Hungarians, refers to them as two lambs among wolves. In a letter dated from Vancluse, August, 1346, he deplores the death of the King, but makes no allusion to the complicity of the Queen.

Boccaccio proclaims her the special pride of Italy, so gracious, gentle, and kindly, that she seemed rather the companion than the queen of her subjects.

Our author cites likewise some of her accusers, and considers most of the current sayings against her as apocryphal. Some of these will not bear quotation in English. Mistral evidently wishes to believe her innocent, and he makes out a pretty good case. He approves the remark of Scipione Ammirato, that she contracted four successive marriages through a desire to have direct heirs. Another notices that had she been dissolute, she would have preferred the liberty of remaining a widow. The poet cites Pope Innocent VI, who gave her the golden rose, and sets great store upon the expression of Saint Catherine of Siena, who calls her "Venerabile madre in Gesù Cristo," and he concludes by saying, "We prefer to concur in the judgment of the good Giannone (1676-1748), which so well agrees with our traditions."

The first act opens with a picture that might tempt a painter of Italian scenes. The Queen and her gay court are seated on the lawn of the palace garden at Naples, overlooking the bay and islands. At the very outset we hear of the Gai Savoir, and the Queen utters the essentially Provençal sentiment that "the chief glory the world should strive for is light, for joy and love are the children of the sun, and art and literature the great torches." She calls upon Anfan of Sisteron to speak to her of her Provence, "the land of God, of song and youth, the finest jewel in her crown," and Anfan, in long and eloquent tirades, tells of Toulouse and Nice and the Isles of Gold, reviews the settling of the Greeks, the domination of the Romans, and the sojourn of the Saracens; Aix and Arles, les Baux, Toulon, are glorified again; we hear of the old liberties of these towns where men sleep, sing, and shout, and of the magnificence of the papal court at Avignon.

> "Enfin, en Avignoun, i'a lou papo! grandour
> Poudé, magnificènci, e poumpo e resplendour,
> Que mestrejon la terro e fan, sènso messorgo,
> Boufa l'alen de Diéu i ribo de la Sorgo."

Lastly, in Avignon, there's the Pope! greatness, power, magnificence, pomp, and splendor, dominating the earth, and without exaggeration, causing the breath of God to blow upon the banks of the Sorgue.

We learn that the brilliancy and animation of the court at Avignon outshine the glories of Rome, and in language that fairly glitters with its high-sounding, highly colored words. We hear of Petrarch and Laura, and the associations of Vaucluse.

At this juncture the Prince arrives, and is struck by the resemblance of the scene to a court of love; he wonders if they are not discussing the question whether love is not drowned in the nuptial holy water font, or whether the lady inspires the lover as much with her presence as when absent. And the Queen defends her mode of life and temperament; she cannot brook the cold and gloomy ways of the north. Were we to apply the methods of Voltaire's strictures of Corneille to this play, it might be interesting to see how many *vers de comédie* could be found in these scenes of dispute between the prince consort and his light-hearted wife.

"A l'avans! zóu! en fèsto arrouinas lou Tresor!"

Go ahead! that's right, ruin the treasury with your feasts!

and to his objections to so many flattering courtiers, the Queen replies:—

"Voulès que moun palais devèngue un mounastié?"

Do you want my palace to become a monastery?

Joanna replies nobly and eloquently to the threats of her husband to assume mastery over her by violent means, and, in spite of the anachronism (the poet makes her use and seemingly invent the term *Renascence*), her defence of the arts and science of her time is forceful and enthusiastic, and carries the reader along. That this sort of eloquence is dramatic, appears, however, rather doubtful.

The next scene interests us more directly in the characters before us. The Prince, left alone with his confidant, Fra Rupert, gives expression to his passionate love for the Queen, and pours forth the bitterness of his soul to see it unrequited. The fierce Hungarian monk denounces, rather justly, it appears to us, the license and levity of the Italian court, and incites Andrea to an appeal to the Pope, "a potentate that has no army, whose dominion extends from pole to pole, who binds and unbinds at his will, upholds, makes, or unmakes thrones as an almighty master."

But Andrea fears the Queen would never pardon him.

"E se noun ai en plen lou mèu si caresso,
L'empèri universal! m'es un gourg d'amaresso!"

And if I have not fully the honey of her caresses
The empire of the world is to me a gulf of bitterness.

Finally the monk and La Catanaise stand alone before us. This woman is the Queen's nurse, who loves her with a fierce sort of passion, and it is she who commits the crime that causes the play to be called a tragedy. This final scene brings out a flood of the most violent vituperation from this veritable virago, some of it exceedingly low in tone. The friar leaves with the threat to have a red-hot nail run through her hellish tongue, and La Catanaise, standing alone, gives vent to her fury in threats of murder.

The next act reveals the Hall of Honor in the Castel-Nuovo at Naples. Andrea in anger proclaims himself king, and in the presence of the Queen and the Italian courtiers gives away one after another all the offices and honors of the realm to his Hungarian followers. A conflict with drawn swords is about to ensue, when the Queen rushes between the would-be combatants, reminding them of the decree of the Pope; but Andrea in fury accuses the Queen of conduct worthy a shameless adventuress, and cites the reports that liken her to Semiramis in her orgies. The Prince of Taranto throws down his glove to the enraged Andrea, who replies by a threat to bring him to the executioner. The Prince of Taranto answers that the executioner may be the supreme law for a king,

> "Mai pèr un qu'a l'ounour dins lou piés e dins l'amo,
> Uno escorno, cousin, se purgo emé la lamo."

> But for one who has honor in his breast and his soul,
> An insult, cousin, is purged with the sword.

Andrea turns to his knights, and leaving the room with them points to the flag bearing the block and axe as emblems. The partisans of Joanna remain full of indignation. La Catanaise addresses them. The Sicilians, she says, waste no time in words, but have a speedier method of punishing a wrong, and she reminds them of the massacre at Palermo. The Prince of Taranto discountenances the proposed crime, for the Queen's fair name would suffer. But the fierce woman points to the flag. "Do you see that axe hanging from a thread? You are all cowards! Let me act alone." And the Prince nobly replies, "Philippine, battles are fought in the sunlight; men of our renown, men of my stamp, do not crouch down in the dark shadow of a plot." And the Catanaise again shows the flag. "Do you see the axe falling upon the block?"

Joanna enters to offer the Prince her thanks for his chivalrous defence of her fair name, and dismisses the other courtiers. The ensuing brief scene between the Queen and the Prince is really very eloquent and very beautiful. The Queen recalls the fact that she was married at nine to Andrea, then only a child too; and she has never known love. The poorest of the shepherdesses on the mountains of Calabria may quench her thirst at the spring, but she, the Queen of the Sun, if to pass away the time, or to have the appearance of happiness, she loves to listen to the echo of song, to behold the joy and brilliancy of a noble fête, her very smile becomes criminal. And the Prince reminds her that she is the Provençal queen, and that in the great times of that people, if the consort were king, love was a god, and he recalls the names of all the ladies made famous by the Troubadours. Thereupon the Queen in an outburst of enthusiasm truly Felibrean invokes the God of Love, the God that slew Dido, and speaks in the spirit of the days of courtly love, "O thou God of Love, hearken unto me. If my fatal beauty is destined sooner or later to bring about my death, let this flame within me be, at least, the pyre that shall kindle the song of the poet! Let my beauty be the luminous star exalting men's hearts to lofty visions!"

The chivalrous Prince is dismissed, and Joanna is alone with, her thoughts. The little page Dragonet sings outside a plaintive song with the refrain:—

> "Que regrèt!
> Jamai digues toun secrèt."

> What regret!
> Never tell thy secret.

La Catanaise endeavors to excite the fears of the Queen, insinuating that the

Pope may give the crown to Andrea. Joanna has no fear.

"We shall have but to appear before the country with this splendor of irresistible grace, and like the smoke borne away by the breeze, suddenly my enemies shall disappear."

We may ask whether such self-praise comes gracefully from the Queen herself, whether she might not be less conscious of her own charm. La Catanaise is again alone on the scene, threatening. "The bow is drawn, the hen setting." This last comparison, the reader will remark, would be simply impossible as the termination of an act in a serious English play. This last scene, too, is wofully weak and purposeless.

The conversation of three courtiers at the beginning of Act III apprises us of the fact that the Pope has succeeded in bringing about a reconciliation between the royal pair, and that they are both to be crowned, and as a matter of precaution, the nurse Philippine, and the monk Fra Rupert are to be sent upon their several ways. The scene is next filled by the conspirators, La Catanaise directing the details of the plots. It is made clear that the Queen is utterly ignorant of these proceedings, which are after all useless; for we fail to see what valid motive these plotters have to urge them on to their contemptible deed. A brilliant banquet scene ensues, wherein Anfan of Sisteron sings a song of seven stanzas about the fairy Mélusine, and seven times Dragonet sings the refrain, "Sian de la raço di lesert" (We are of the race of the lizards). And there are enthusiastic tirades in praise of the Queen and of Provence, and all is merry. But Andrea spills salt upon the table, which evil augury seems to be taken seriously. This little episode is foolish, and unwrorthy of a tragedy. We are on the verge of an assassination. Either the gloomy forebodings and the terror of the event should be impressed upon us, or the exaggerated gayety and high spirits of the revellers should by contrast make the coming event seem more terrible; but the spilling of salt is utterly trivial. After the feast La Catanaise and her daughter proceed to their devilish work, in the room now lighted only by the pale rays of the moon, while the voice of the screech-owl is heard outside. The trap is set for the King; he is strangled just out of sight with the silken noose. The Queen is roused by her nurse. The palace is in an uproar, and the act terminates with a passionate demand for vengeance and justice on the part of Fra Rupert.

And now the Fourth Act. Here Mistral is in his element; here his love of rocky landscapes, of azure seas and golden islands, of song and festivity, finds full play. The tragedy is forgotten, the dramatic action completely interrupted,—never mind. We accompany the Queen on her splendid galley all the way from Naples to Marseilles. She leaves amid the acclamations of the Neapolitans, recounts the splendors of the beautiful bay, and promises to return "like the star of night coming out of the mist, laurel in hand, on the white wings of her Provençal galley." The boat starts, the rowers sing their plaintive rhythmic songs, the Queen is enraptured by the beauty of the fleeing shores, the white sail glistens in the glorious blue above. She is lulled by the motion of the boat and the waving of the hangings of purple and gold. Midway on her journey she receives a visit from the Infante of Majorca, James of Aragon, who seems to be wandering over that part of the sea; then the astrologer Anselme predicts her marriage with *Alio* and her death.

She shall be visited with the sins of her ancestors; the blood spilled by Charles of Anjou cries for vengeance. The Queen passes through a moment of gloom. She dispels it, exclaiming: "Be it so, strike where thou wilt, O fate, I am a queen; I shall fight, if need be, until death, to uphold my cause and my womanly honor. If my wild planet is destined to sink in a sea of blood and tears, the glittering trace I shall leave on the earth will show at least that I was worthy to be thy great queen, O brilliant Provence!"

She descends into the ship, and the rowers resume their song. Later we arrive at Nice, where the Queen is received by an exultant throng. She forgets the awful predictions and is utterly filled with delight. She will visit all the cities where she is loved, her ambition is to see her flag greeted all along the Mediterranean with shouts of joy and love. She feels herself to be a Provençale. "Come, people, here I am; breathe me in, drink me in! It is sweet to me to be yours, and sweet to please you; and you may gaze in love and admiration upon me, for I am your queen!"

The journey is resumed. We pass the Isles of Gold, and the raptures are renewed. At Marseilles the Queen is received by the Consuls, and swears solemnly to respect all the rights, customs, and privileges of the land, and the Consul exacts as the last oath that she swear to see that the noble speech of Arles shall be maintained and spoken in the land of Provence. The act closes with the sentiment, "May Provence triumph in every way!"

The last act brings us to the great hall of the papal palace at Avignon, where the Pope is to pronounce judgment upon the Queen. Fra Rupert, disguised as a pilgrim, harangues the throng, and two Hungarian knights are beaten in duel by Galéas of Mantua. This duel, with its alternate cries of Dau! Dau! Tè! Tè! Zóu! Zóu! is difficult to take seriously and reminds us of Tartarin. The Queen enters in conversation with Petrarch. The Hungarian knights utter bitter accusations against the Queen, who gives them in place of iron chains the golden chains about her neck, whereupon the knights gallantly declare their hearts are won forever. The doors open at the back and we see the papal court. Bertrand des Baux gives a hideous account of the torture and death of those who had a hand in the death of Andrea. The Queen makes a long speech, expressing her deep grief at the calumnies and slander that beset her. The court and people resolve themselves into a kind of opera chorus, expressing their various sentiments in song. The Queen next reviews her life with Andrea, and concludes:—

"And it seemed to me noble and worthy of a queen to melt with a glance the cold of the frost, to make the almond tree blossom with a smile, to be amiable to all, affable, generous, and lead my people with a thread of wool! Yes, all the thought of my mad youth was to be loved and to reign by the power of love. Who could have foretold that, afterward, on the day of the great disaster, all this should be made a reproach against me! that I should be accused, at the age of twenty, of instigating an awful crime!"

And she breaks down weeping. The page, the people, the pilgrim, and the astrologer again sing in a sort of operatic ensemble their various emotions. The Pope absolves the Queen, the pilgrim denounces the verdict furiously, and is put to death by Galéas of Mantua. So ends the play.

La Rèino Jano is a pageant rather than a tragedy. It is full of song and sunshine, glow and glitter. The characters all talk in the exaggerated and exuberant style of Mistral, who is not dramatist enough to create independent being, living before us. The central personage is in no sense a tragic character. The fanatical Fra Rupert and the low, vile-tongued Catanaise are not tragic characters. The psychology throughout is decidedly upon the surface.

The author in his introduction warns us that to judge this play we must place ourselves at the point of view of the Provençals, in whom many an expression or allusion that leaves the ordinary reader or spectator untouched, will possibly awaken, as he hopes, some particular emotion. This is true of all his literature; the Provençal language, the traditions, the memories of Provence, are the web and woof of it all.

It is interesting to note the impression made by the language upon a Frenchman and a critic of the rank of Jules Lemaître. He says in concluding his review of this play: —

"The language is too gay, it has too much sing-song, it is too harmonious. It does not possess the rough gravity of the Spanish, and has too few of the *i*'s and *e*'s that soften the sonority of the Italian. I may venture to say it is too expressive, too full of onomatopœia. Imagine a language, in which to say, "He bursts out laughing," one must use the word *s'escacalasso*! There are too many *on*'s and *oun*'s and too much *ts* and *dz* in the pronunciation. So that the Provençal language, in spite of everything, keeps a certain patois vulgarity. It forces the poet, so to say, to perpetual song-making. It must be very difficult, in that language, to have an individual style, still more difficult to express abstract ideas. But it is a merry language."

The play has never yet been performed, and until a trial is made, one is inclined to think it would not be effective, except as a spectacle. It is curious that the Troubadours produced no dramatic literature whatever, and that the same lack is found in the modern revival.

Aubanel's *Lou Pan dóu Pecat* (The Bread of Sin), written in 1863, and performed in 1878 at Montpellier, seems to have been successful, and was played at Paris at the Théâtre Libre in 1888, in the verse-translation made by Paul Arène. Aubanel wrote two other plays, *Lou Pastre*, which is lost, and *Lou Raubatòn*, a work that must be considered unfinished. Two plays, therefore, constitute the entire dramatic production in the new language.

PART THIRD

CONCLUSIONS

It would be idle to endeavor to determine whether Mistral is to be classed as a great poet, or whether the Félibres have produced a great literature, and nothing is defined when the statement is made that Mistral is or is not a great poet. His genius may be said to be limited geographically, for if from it were eliminated all that pertains directly to Provence, the remainder would be almost nothing. The only human nature known to the poet is the human nature of Provence, and while it is perfectly true that a human being in Provence could be typical of human nature in general, and arouse interest in all men through his humanity common to all, the fact is, that Mistral has not sought to express what is of universal interest, but has invariably chosen to present human life in its Provençal aspects and from one point of view only. A second limitation is found in the unvarying exteriority of his method of presenting human nature. Never does he probe deeply into the souls of his Provençals. Very vividly indeed does he reproduce their words and gestures; but of the deeper under-currents, the inner conflicts, the agonies of doubt and indecision, the bitterness of disappointments, the lofty aspirations toward a higher inner life or a closer communion with the universe, the moral problems that shake a human soul, not a syllable. Nor is he a poet who pours out his own soul into verse.

External nature is for him, again, nature as seen in Provence. The rocks and trees, the fields and the streams, do not awaken in him a stir of emotions because of their power to compel a mood in any responsive poetic soul, but they excite him primarily as the rocks and trees, the fields and streams of his native region. He is no mere word-painter. Rarely do his descriptions appear to exist for their own sake. They furnish a necessary, fitting, and delightful background to the action of his poems. They are too often indications of what a Provençal ought to consider admirable or wonderful, they are sometimes spoiled by the poet's excessive partiality for his own little land. His work is ever the work of a man with a mission.

There is no profound treatment of the theme of love. Each of the long poems and his play have a love story as the centre of interest, but the lovers are usually children, and their love utterly without complications. There is everywhere a lovely purity, a delightful simplicity, a straightforward naturalness that is very charming, but in this theme as in the others, Mistral is incapable of tragic depths and heights. So it is as regards the religious side of man's nature. The poet's work is filled with allusions to religion; there are countless legends concerning saints and hermits, descriptions of churches and the papal palace, there is the detailed history of the conversion of Provence to Christianity, but the deepest religious spirit is not his. Only twice in all his work do we come upon a profounder religious sense, in the second half of *Lou Prègo-Diéu* and in *Lou Saume de la Penitènci*. There is no doubt that Mistral is a believer, but religious feeling has not a large place in his work; there are no other meditations upon death and destiny.

And this *âme du Midi, spirit of Provence*, the genius of his race that he has striven to express, what is it? How shall it be defined or formulated? Alphonse Daudet, who knew it, and loved it, whose Parisian life and world-wide success did not destroy in him the love of his native Provence, who loved the very food of the Midi above all others, and jumped up in joy when a southern intonation struck his ear, and who was continually beset with longings to return to the beloved region, has well defined it. He was the friend of Mistral and followed the poet's efforts and achievements with deep and affectionate interest. It is not difficult to see that the satire in the "Tartarin" series is not unkind, nor is it untrue. Daudet approved of the Félibrige movement, though what he himself wrote in Provençal is insignificant. He believed that the national literature could be best vivified by those who most loved their homes, that the best originality could thus be attained. He has said:[17] —

"The imagination of the southerners differs from that of the northerners in that it does not mingle the different elements and forms in literature, and remains lucid in its outbreaks. In our most complex natures you never encounter the entanglement of directions, relations, and figures that characterizes a Carlyle, a Browning, or a Poe. For this reason the man of the north always finds fault with the man of the south for his lack of depth and darkness.

"If we consider the most violent of human passions, love, we see that the southerner makes it the great affair of his life, but does not allow himself to become disorganized. He likes the talk that goes with it, its lightness, its change. He hates the slavery of it. It furnishes a pretext for serenades, fine speeches, light scoffing, caresses. He finds it difficult to comprehend the joining together of love and death, which lies in the northern nature, and casts a shade of melancholy upon these brief delights."

Daudet notes the ease with which the southerner is carried away and duped by the mirage of his own fancy, his semi-sincerity in excitement and enthusiasm. He admired the natural eloquence of his Provençals. He found a justification for their exaggerations.

"Is it right to accuse a man of lying, who is intoxicated with his own eloquence, who, without evil intent, or love of deceit, or any instinct of scheming or false trading, seeks to embellish his own life, and other people's, with stories he knows to be illusions, but which he wishes were true? Is Don Quixote a liar? Are all the poets deceivers who aim to free us from realities, to go soaring off into space? After all, among southerners, there is no deception. Each one, within himself, restores things to their proper proportions."

Daudet had Mistral's love of the sunshine. He needed it to inspire him. He believed it explained the southern nature.

Concerning the absence of metaphysics in the race he says: —

[17] See *Revue de Paris*, 15 avril, 1898.

"These reasonings may culminate in a state of mind such as we see extolled in Buddhism, a colorless state, joyless and painless, across which the fleeting splendors of thought pass like stars. Well, the man of the south cares naught for that sort of paradise. The vein of real sensation is freely, perpetually open, open to life. The side that pertains to abstraction, to logic, is lost in mist."

We have referred to the power of story-telling among the Provençals and their responsiveness as listeners. Daudet mentions the contrast to be observed between an audience of southerners and the stolid, self-contained attitude of a crowd in the north.

The evil side of the southern temperament, the faults that accompany these traits, are plainly stated by the great novelist. Enthusiasm turns to hypocrisy, or brag; the love of what glitters, to a passion for luxury at any cost; sociability, the desire to please, become weakness and fulsome flattery. The orator beats his breast, his voice is hoarse, choked with emotion, his tears flow conveniently, he appeals to patriotism and the noblest sentiments. There is a legend, according to Daudet, which says that when Mirabeau cried out, "We will not leave unless driven out at the point of the bayonet," a voice off at one side corrected the utterance, murmuring sarcastically, "And if the bayonets come, we make tracks!"

The southerner, when he converses, is roused to animation readily. His eye flashes, his words are uttered with strong intonations, the impressiveness of a quiet, earnest, self-contained manner is unknown to him.

Daudet is a novelist and a humorist. Mistral is a poet; hence, although he professes to aim at a full expression of the "soul of his Provence," there are many aspects of the Provençal nature that he has not touched upon. He has omitted all the traits that lend themselves to satirical treatment, and, although he is in many ways a remarkable realist, he has very little dramatic power, and seems to lack the gift of searching analysis of individual character. It is hardly fair to reckon it as a shortcoming in the poet and apostle of Provence that he presents only what is most beautiful in the life about him. The novelist offers us a faithful and vivid image of the men of his own day. The poet glorifies the past, clings to tradition, and exhorts his countrymen to return to it.

Essentially and above all else a conservative, Mistral has the gravest doubts about so-called modern progress. Undoubtedly honest in desiring the well-being of his fellow Provençals, he believes that this can be preserved or attained only by a following of tradition. There must be no breaking with the past. Daudet, late in life, adhered to this doctrine. His son quotes him as saying:—

"I am following, with gladness, the results of the impulse Mistral has given. Return to tradition! that is our salvation in the present going to pieces. I have always felt this instinctively. It came to me clearly only a few years ago. It is a bad thing to become wholly loosened from the soil, to forget the village church spire. Curiously enough poetry attaches only to objects that have come down to us, that have had long use. What is called *progress*, a vague and very doubtful term, rouses the lower parts of our intelligence. The higher parts vibrate the better for what has moved and inspired a long series of imaginative minds, inheriting each from a predecessor, strengthened by the sight of the same landscapes, by the same perfumes, by the touch of the same furniture, polished by wear. Very ancient impressions sink into the depth of that obscure memory which we may call the *race-memory*, out of which is woven the mass of individual memories."

Mistral is truly the poet of the Midi. One can best see how superior he is as an artist in words by comparing him with the foremost of his fellow-poets. He is a master of language. He has the eloquence, the enthusiasm, the optimism of his race. His poetic earnestness saves his tendency to exaggerate. His style, in all its superiority, is a southern style, full of interjections, full of long, sonorous words. His thought, his expressions, are ever lucid. His art is almost wholly objective. His work has extraordinary unity, and therefore does not escape the monotony that was unavoidable when the poet voluntarily limited himself to a single purpose in life, and to treatment of the themes thereunto pertaining. Believers in material progress, those who look for great changes in political and social conditions, will turn from Mistral with indifference. His contentment with present things, and his love of the past, are likely to irritate them. Those who seek in a poet consolation in the personal trials of life, a new message concerning human destiny, a new note in the everlasting themes that the great poets have sung, will be disappointed.

A word must be said of him as a writer of French. In the earlier years he felt the weight of the Academy. He did not feel that French would allow full freedom. He was scrupulous and timid. He soon shook off this timidity and became a really remarkable wielder of the French tongue. His translations of his own works have doubtless reached a far wider public than the works themselves, and are certainly characterized by great boldness, clearness, and an astonishingly large vocabulary.

His earlier work is clearly inspired by his love of Greek literature, and those qualities in Latin literature wherein the Greek genius shines through, possibly also by some mysterious affinity with the Greek spirit resulting from climate or atavism. This never entirely left him. When later he writes of Provence in the Middle Age, of the days of the Troubadours, his manner does not change; his work offers no analogies here with the French Romantic school.

No poet, it would seem, was ever so in love with his own language; no artist ever so loved the mere material he was using. Mistral loves the words he uses, he loves their sound, he loves to hear them from the lips of those about him; he loves the intonations and the cadences of his verse; his love is for the speech itself aside from any meaning it conveys. A beautiful instrument it is indeed. Possibly nothing is more peculiarly striking about him than this extreme enthusiasm for his golden speech, his *lengo d'or*.

To him must be conceded the merit of originality, great originality. In seeking the source of many of his conceptions, one is led to the conclusion, and his own testimony bears it out, that they are the creations of his own fancy. If there is much prosaic realism in the *Poem of the Rhone*, the Prince and the Anglore are purely the children of Mistral's almost naïve imagination, and Calendau and Esterello are attached to the real world of history by the slenderest bonds. When we seek for resemblances between his conceptions and those of other poets, we can undoubtedly find them. Mireille now and then reminds of Daphnis and Chloe, of Hermann and Dorothea, of Evangeline, but the differences are far more in evidence than the resemblances. Esterello is in an attitude toward Calendau not without analogy to that of Beatrice toward Dante, but it would be impossible to find at any point the slightest imitation of Dante. Some readers have been reminded of Faust in reading *Nerto*, but beyond the scheme of the Devil to secure a woman's soul, there is little similarity. Nothing could be more utterly without philosophy than *Nerto*. Mistral has drawn his inspirations from within himself; he has not worked over the poems and legends of former poets, or sought much of his subject-matter in the productions of former ages. He has not suffered from the deep reflection, the pondering, and the doubt that destroy originality.

If Mistral had written his poems in French, he would certainly have stood apart from the general line of French poets. It would have been impossible to attach him to any of the so-called "schools" of poetry that have followed one another during this century in France. He is as unlike the Romantics as he is unlike the Parnassians. M. Brunetière would find no difficulty in applying to his work the general epithet of "social" that so well characterizes French literature considered in its main current, for Mistral always sings to his fellow-men to move them, to persuade them, to stir their hearts. Almost all of his poems in the lyrical form show him as the spokesman of his fellows or as the leader urging them to action. He is therefore not of the school of "Art for Art's sake," but his art is consecrated to the cause he represents.

His thought is ever pure and high; his lessons are lessons of love, of noble aims, of energy and enthusiasm. He is full of love for the best in the past, love of his native soil, love of his native landscapes, love of the men about him, love of his country. He is a poet of the "Gai Saber," joyous and healthy, he has never felt a trace of the bitterness, the disenchantment, the gloom and the pain of a Byron or a Leopardi. He is eminently representative of the race he seeks to glorify in its own eyes and in the world's, himself a type of that race at its very best, with all its exuberance and energy, with its need of outward manifestation, life and movement. An important place must be assigned to him among those who have bodied forth their poetic conceptions in the various euphonious forms of speech descended from the ancient speech of Rome.

In Provence, and far beyond its borders, he is known and loved. His activity has not ceased. His voice is still heard, clear, strong, hopeful, inspiring. *Mireille* is sung in the ruined Roman theatre at Aries, museums are founded to preserve Provençal art and antiquities, the Felibrean feasts continue with unabated enthusiasm. Mistral's life is a successful life; he has revived a language, created a literature, inspired a people. So potent is art to-day in the old land of the Troubadours. All the charm and beauty of that sunny land, all that is enchanting in its past, all the best, in the ideal sense, that may be hoped for in its future, is expressed in his musical, limpid, lovely verse. Such a poet and such a leader of men is rare in the annals of literature. Such complete oneness of purpose and of achievement is rare among men.

APPENDIX: TRANSLATION OF THE PSALM OF PENITENCE

We offer here a literal prose translation of the *Psalm of Penitence*.

THE PSALM OF PENITENCE

I

Lord, at last thy wrath hurleth its thunderbolts upon our foreheads, and in the night our vessel strikes its prow against the rocks.

Lord, thou cuttest us down with the sword of the barbarian like fine wheat, and not one of the cravens that we shielded comes to our defence.

Lord, thou twistest us like a willow wand, thou breakest down to-day all our pride; there is none to envy us, who but yesterday were so proud.

Lord, our land goeth to ruin in war and strife; and if thou withhold thy mercy, great and small will devour one another.

Lord, thou art terrible, thou strikest us upon the back; in awful turmoil thou breakest our power, compelling us to confess past evil.

II

Lord, we had strayed away from the austerity of the old laws and ways. Virtues, domestic customs, we had destroyed and demolished.

Lord, giving an evil example, and denying thee like the heathen, we had one day closed up thy temples and mocked thy Holy Christ.

Lord, leaving behind us thy sacraments and commandments, we had brutally lost belief in all but self-interest and progress!

Lord, in the waste heavens we have clouded thy light with our smoke, and to-day the sons mock the nakedness and purity of their fathers.

Lord, we have blown upon thy Bible with the breath of false knowledge; and holding ourselves up like the poplar trees, we wretched beings have declared ourselves gods.

Lord, we have left the furrow, we have trampled all respect under foot; and with the heavy wine that intoxicates us we defile the innocent.

III

Lord, we are thy prodigal children, but we are thy Christians of old; let thy justice chastise us, but give us not over unto death.

Lord, in the name of so many brave men, who went forth fearless, valiant, docile, grave, and then fell in battle;

Lord, in the name of so many mothers, who are about to pray to God for their sons, and who next year, alas! and the year thereafter, shall see them no more;

Lord, in the name of so many women who have at their bosoms a little child, and who, poor creatures, moisten the earth and the sheets of their beds with tears;

Lord, in the name of the poor, in the name of the strong, in the name of the dead who shall die for their country, their duty, and their faith;

Lord, for so many defeats, so many tears and woes, for so many towns ravaged, for so much brave, holy blood;

Lord, for so many adversities, for so much mourning throughout our France, for so many insults upon our heads;

IV

Lord, disarm thy justice. Cast down thine eye upon us, and heed the cries of the bruised and wounded!

Lord, if the rebellious cities, through their luxury and folly, have overturned the scale-pan of thy balance, resisting and denying thee;

Lord, before the breath of the Alps, that praiseth God winter and summer, all the trees of the fields, obedient, bow together;

Lord, France and Provence have sinned only through forgetfulness; do thou forgive us our offences, for we repent of the evil of former days.

Lord, we desire to become men, thou canst set us free. We are Gallo-Romans, and of noble race, and we walk upright in our land.

Lord, we are not the cause of the evil, send down upon us a ray of peace. Lord, help our cause, and we shall live again and love thee.

THE PRESENT CAPOULIÉ OF THE FÉLIBRIGE.

M. Pierre Devoluy, of the town of Die, was elected at Arles, in April, 1901. The Consistory was presided over by Mistral.

BIBLIOGRAPHY

The following list contains the most important works that have been published concerning Mistral and the Félibrige. Numerous articles have appeared in nearly all the languages of Europe in various magazines. Of these only such are mentioned as seem worthy of special notice.

WORKS CONCERNING THE FÉLIBRIGE IN GENERAL

America

JANVIER, THOMAS A., Numerous articles in the Century Magazine, New York, 1893, and following years.

An Embassy to Provence. New York, 1893.

PRESTON, HARRIETT, *Mistral's Calendau*. The Atlantic Monthly, New York, 1874.

Aubanel's Miòugrano entreduberto. The Atlantic Monthly, New York, 1874.

England

CRAIG, DUNCAN, *Miéjour Provençal Legend, Life, Language, and Literature*. London.

The Handbook of the Modern Provençal Language.

CROMBIE, J.W., *The Poets and Peoples of Foreign Lands: Frédéric Mistral*. Elliot, London, 1890.

HARTOG, CECIL, *Poets of Provence*. London Contemporary Review, 1894.

France

BOISSIN, FIRMIN, *Le Midi littéraire contemporain*. Douladoure, Toulouse, 1887.

DE BOUCHAUD, *Roumanille et le Félibrige*. Mougin, Lyons, 1896.

BRUN, C., *L'Evolution félibréenne*. Paquet, Lyons, 1896.

DONNADIEU, F., *Les Précurseurs des Félibres*. Quantin, Paris, 1888.

HENNION, C., *Les Fleurs félibresques*. Paris, 1893.

JOURDANNE, G., *Histoire du Félibrige*. Roumanille, Avignon, 1897.

LINTILHAC, E., *Les Félibres à travers leur monde et leur poésie*. Lemerre, Paris, 1895.

Précis de la littérature française. Paris, 1890.

LEGRÉ, L., *Le Poète Théodore Aubanel*. Paris, 1894.

MARGON, A. DE, *Les Précurseurs des Félibres*. Béziers, 1891.

MARIÉTON, PAUL, *La Terre provençale*. Lemerre, Paris, 1894.

Article *Félibrige* in the *Grande Encyclopédie*.

Article *Mistral* in the *Grande Encyclopédie*.

MICHEL, S., *La Petite Patrie*. Roumanille, Avignon, 1894.

NOULET, B., *Essai sur l'histoire littéraire des patois du midi de la France, aux VIIIe siécle*. Montpellier, 1877.

PARIS, GASTON, *Penseurs et poètes*. Calmann-Lévy, Paris, 1896.

RESTORI, *Histoire de la littérature provençale depuis les temps les plus reculés jusqu'à nos jours*. Montpellier, 1895. (Translated from the Italian.)

ROQUE-FERRIER, A., *Mélanges de critique littéraire et de philologie*. Montpellier, 1892.

SAINT-RENÉ-TAILLANDIER, V., *Etudes littéraires*. Plon et Cie, Paris, 1881.

TAVERNIER, E., *La Renaissance provençale et Roumanille*. Gervais, Paris, 1884.

Le mouvement littéraire provençal et Lis Isclo d'Or de Frédéric Mistral. Aix, 1876.

DE TERRIS, J., *Roumanille et la littérature provençale*. Blond, Paris, 1894.

DE VINAC, M., *Les Félibres*. Richaud, Gap, 1882.

Germany

BÖHMER, E., *Die provenzalische Dichtung der Gegenwart*. Heilbronn, 1870.

KOSCHWITZ, E., *Ueber die provenzalischen Feliber und ihre Vorgänger*. Berlin, 1894.

Grammaire historique de la langue des Félibres. Greifswald and Paris,

1894.

A study of Bertuch's translation of Nerto in the *Litteraturblatt für germanische und romanische Philologie*. 1892.

A study of Provençal phonetics with a translation of the *Cant dóu Soulèu. Sonderabdruck aus der Zeitschrift für französische Sprache und Litteratur*. Berlin, 1893.

SCHNEIDER, B., *Bemerkungen zur litterarischen Bewegung auf neuprovenzalischem Sprachgebiete*. Berlin, 1887.

WELTER, N., *Frederi Mistral, der Dichter der Provence*. Marburg, 1899.[18]

Italy

LICER, MARIA, *I Felibri*, in the *Roma letteraria*. June, 1893.

PORTAL, E., *Appunti letterari: Sulla poesia provenzale*. Pedone, Palermo, 1890.

La Letteratura provenzale moderna. Reber, Palermo, 1893.

Scritti vari di letteratura classica provenzale moderna. Reber, Palermo, 1895.

RESTORI, A., *Letteratura provenzale*. Hoepli, Milan, 1892.

ZUCCARO, L., *Un avvenimento letterario; Mistral tragico in the Scena illustrata*. Florence, 1891.

Il Felibrigio, rinascimento delle lettere provenzali, Concordia. Novara, 1892.

Spain

TUBINO, *Historia del renacimiento literario contemporaneo en Cataluña, Baleares y Valencia*. Madrid, 1881.

MISTRAL'S WORKS

Mirèio. 1859.

Calendau. Avignon, 1867. Paris, Lemerre, 1887.

Lis Isclo d'Or. 1876.

Nerto. Hachette, Paris, 1884.

Lou Tresor dóu Fébrige. Aix, 1886.

La Rèino Jano. Lemerre, Paris, 1890.

---

[18] The present work was completed in manuscript before the reception of Welter's book.

Lou Pouèmo dóu Rose. Lemerre, Paris, 1897.

TRANSLATIONS OF MISTRAL'S WORKS

H. GRANT, *An English Version of F. Mistral's Mirèio from the Original Provençal.* London.

HARRIETT PRESTON, *Mistral's Mirèio. A Provençal Poem Translated.* Roberts Bros., Boston, 1872. Second edition, 1891.

A. BERTUCH, *Der Trommler von Arcole.* Deutsche Dichtung, Dresden, 1890.

Nerto. Trübner, Strassburg, 1890.

Mirèio. Trübner, Strassburg, 1892.

Espouscado. Zeitschrift für französische Sprache und Litteratur, XV², p. 267.

HENNION, *Mireille.* Traduction en vers français.

E. RIGAUD, *Mireille.* Metrical translation into French, with the original form of stanza.

JAROSLAV VRCHLICHKY. Translation of several poems of Mistral into Bohemian, under the title, *Z básni Mistralovych,* in the Review, *Kvety.* Prague, 1886.

Hostem u Basniku. Prague, 1891. Contains seven poems by Aubanel and thirteen by Mistral.

DOM SIGISMOND BOUSKA, *Le Tambour d'Arcole,* in the Review, *Lumir.* Prague, 1893.

Cantos IV and V of *Mirèio,* in the Review, *Vlast.* Prague, 1894.

PELAY BOIZ, *Mirèio,* in Catalan.

ROCA Y ROCA, *Calendau.* Lo Gay Saber, Barcelona, 1868.

C. BARALLAT Y FALGUERA, *Mireya, poema provenzal de Frederico Mistral puesto en prosa española.*

MARIA LICER, *L'Angelo* (Canto VI of *Nerto*). Italian. Iride, Casal, 1889.

A. NAUM, *Traduceri.* Jassy, 1891. (Translation into Rumanian of Canto IV of *Mirèio, The Song of Magali,* and *The Drummer of Arcole.*)

T. CANNIZZARO, *La Venere d'Arli,* in *Vita Intima.* Milan, 1891.

INDEX

Lector House believes that a society develops through a two-fold approach of continuous learning and adaptation, which is derived from the study of classic literary works spread across the historic timeline of literature records. Therefore, we aim at reviving, repairing and redeveloping all those inaccessible or damaged but historically as well as culturally important literature across subjects so that the future generations may have an opportunity to study and learn from past works to embark upon a journey of creating a better future.

This book is a result of an effort made by Lector House towards making a contribution to the preservation and repair of original ancient works which might hold historical significance to the approach of continuous learning across subjects.

HAPPY READING & LEARNING!

LECTOR HOUSE LLP
E-MAIL: lectorpublishing@gmail.com